1 0   S T E P S   T O

Successful
Business Writing

Jack E. Appleman

ASTD
PRESS

Alexandria, Virginia

ASTD Press is an internationally renowned source of insightful and practical information on workplace learning and performance topics, including training basics, evaluation and return-on-investment (ROI), instructional systems development (ISD), e-learning, leadership, and career development.

Ordering information: Books published by ASTD Press can be purchased by visiting our website at store.astd.org or by calling 800.628.2783 or 703.683.8100.

Library of Congress Control Number: 2007921487

ISBN-10: 1-56286-481-5
ISBN-13: 978-1-56286-481-1

ASTD Press Editorial Staff
Director: Cat Russo
Manager, Acquisitions & Author Relations: Mark Morrow
Editorial Manager: Jacqueline Edlund-Braun
Editorial Assistant: Maureen Soyars
Retail Trade Manager: Yelba Quinn
Copyeditor: Christine Cotting
Indexer: April Davis
Interior Design and Production: UpperCase Publication Services, Ltd.
Cover Design: Kristi Sone

Printed by Victor Graphics, Inc., Baltimore, Maryland, www.victorgraphics.com.

CONTENTS

Let's face it, most people spend their days in chaotic, fast-paced, time- and resource-strained organizations. Finding time for just one more project, assignment, or even learning opportunity—no matter how career enhancing or useful—is difficult to imagine. The *10 Steps* series is designed for today's busy professional who needs advice and guidance on a wide array of topics ranging from project management to people management, from business planning strategy to decision making and time management, from return-on-investment to conducting organizational surveys and questionnaires. Each book in this ASTD series promises to take its readers on a journey to basic understanding, with practical application the ultimate destination. This is truly a just-tell-me-what-to-do-now series. You will find action-driven language teamed with examples, worksheets, case studies, and tools to help you quickly implement the right steps and chart a path to your own success. The *10 Steps* series will appeal to a broad business audience from middle managers to upper-level management. Workplace learning and human resource professionals along with other professionals seeking to improve their value proposition in their organizations will find these books a great resource.

PREFACE

Today, we're all writers. Gone, for the most part, are the days when executives dictated letters to secretaries. The vast majority of us write our own documents, thanks to personal computers and email communication, which enable us to create and deliver messages quickly. We generate more documents than ever before—*but we don't do it well.*

Study after study point to an inadequate level of writing in the business world. Still, writing typically has been viewed as one of those soft skills that would be nice for employees to improve but not worth the investment of time or money. The prevailing attitude in most companies has been, "If we can't measure the benefits in dollars and cents, then why do it?" Most companies are more likely to invest in training for sales, project management, budgeting, and other skills that are easier to link to the bottom line than is business writing.

Recently, however, some employers have started to get it: poor writing equals low productivity. The latest studies reveal that employees who write poorly waste countless hours and, more important, countless dollars. These findings have prompted U.S. companies to spend billions of dollars on writing instruction each year.

The good news is that business writing is a *learned skill* based on fundamental principles like clarity, conciseness, and organization. It doesn't matter how extensive your vocabulary is or what grades you received in high school or college English. If you can learn to convey a message simply—so readers quickly get it—then you can become an effective business writer.

Upgrading writing skills will pay off for you and for employees at every level, from owners and top executives to middle managers and administrative assistants. Those who learn to write better will work more productively and be able to demonstrate leadership and management abilities. That's why companies and not-for-profit organizations of all sizes should look at ways to improve employees' writing skills—through tactics such as group workshops, one-on-one coaching, standard writing styles and templates for frequently written documents, and printed or online resources.

A good place to start, whether you're a decision maker or just a working professional, is with *10 Steps to Successful Business Writing,* which summarizes the most critical skills for the business writer. Learn these skills and commit to applying them in your documents—and you can improve your writing and your productivity dramatically. It's that simple.

Acknowledgments

Thanks to my wife Rosa for her love, for her strong moral support, and for handling even more household responsibilities during this yearlong project when I spent so many nights stuck in the office, writing. And thanks to my daughters Gail and Sarah for their love, for their support, and for making Rosa and me proud parents.

Jack E. Appleman
January 2008

INTRODUCTION

Successful business writing starts with simplicity. The beauty of simplicity is that it can produce results faster.

A few years ago, a technology firm produced a television commercial for its software consulting services that went something like this: One man (we'll call him Bob) is speaking in complex technical jargon to explain to another man (let's call him Dave) why their firm should invest in a particular software package. Frustrated with words he doesn't understand, Dave implores Bob to cut the techno-babble and explain the purchase rationale in a way that management could understand. Bob pauses to think about his words; then he says, "For every buck we invest, we'll get back two." So simple, so quick, and so powerful!

Think of some of the most memorable advertising slogans:
- Nike: "Just do it."
- State Farm: "Like a good neighbor, State Farm is there."
- Subway: "Eat fresh."

Those slogans are all so simple, but the advertising agency creative teams probably spent many months and big bucks developing them. Simple isn't always easy. It's like hitting a golf ball: one of the most important skills is—simply—keeping your head down during the swing, but so many golfers can't do it consistently.

The good news is that effective business writing doesn't demand that we brainstorm clever slogans or acquire hand-eye coordination. It requires only that we know what we want to say and then choose simple words and follow simple rules.

Why is it so hard to be simple? Too bad that all messages can't be as direct as that TV commercial or those popular slogans. Consider these messages I recently received while battling my personal computer:

1. *Avsynmgr has caused an error in MCSCAN32DLL. The application will close.*

   Oh, I get it. I knew I should have paid more attention to my *Avsynmgr!*

2. *The instruction at 0xSad715131 referenced memory at 0x0000019. The memory could not be found.*

   I knew it. I should've referenced that memory at 0x0000019 like I usually do!

3. *The application Windows Genuine Advantage Notification has changed since you first gave it access to the Internet. Do you still want to let it access the Internet?*

   I want to access the Internet and don't care if Windows Blah-Blah-Blah can access it!

These messages may be perfectly clear to you—if you're the information technology director—but not to me. I even had trouble downloading my favorite jazz radio station online to help get me through the long hours writing this book. Sure, I figured it out eventually, but I still crave simple instructions.

On the bright side, technology and software companies are starting to recognize that we plain folk need plain instructions—with no chance for confusion. Microsoft has managed to craft a brilliantly direct message that appears on my screen after I close all the programs: *It is now safe to turn off your computer.* Hallelujah! There's the beauty of using plain English.

What You'll Find in This Book

This book is written for people at all levels of writing proficiency, including those who struggled with high school or college English.

Not having a rich vocabulary actually could help you become a more effective business writer because you automatically go for the simpler language. That's good!

I've put together what I believe are the 10 most important steps for successful writing in the simplest way, and I've included an appendix that explains how companies and organizations can improve employees' writing skills.

If you're looking for a book with extensive discussion on the philosophy of writing, audience analysis, readability matrixes, sentence diagrams, and countless grammar rules, this isn't it. I didn't have the patience to go into such detail—and my gut feeling was that you wouldn't have the patience to read it. Instead, I wrote a *short, practical guide to help you write better.*

Because the best way to improve your writing is by actual practice—rather than by learning a theory—I've chosen to explain by example. Throughout the 10 steps you'll find many places where I've presented the same message in two ways—one version better than the other. Taking the principle of powerful simplicity, here's a preview:

◆ **Wordy:** *Many topics were discussed at the meeting held yesterday at 11 in the morning. Among the most pressing topics was the high travel costs among the salesforce, which are becoming more and more of a problem. It's gotten to the point that the CEO has said unequivocally that our division must conduct a teleconference with the salesforce. This means we have to cancel the next regional sales meeting that was previously scheduled. The CEO and other senior executives have determined that this would help save on travel, which has become way too costly.*

◆ **Simple:** *To reduce travel costs, the CEO has ordered us to cancel the next regional sales meeting and conduct a teleconference instead.*

Many of the tips I'll give you here were collected from my business writing workshops over the past few years. Feedback from students I've taught in group and one-on-one sessions helped me identify the most important skills to address and the most critical types of documents to include in Step 10: Master the Documents You Use Most Often.

If you have interest in or responsibility for the collective writing abilities of the employees in your organization, the Appendix explains practices to enhance the writing of personnel at all levels and shows you how to design and conduct writing training tailored to your employees' needs.

Here are the 10 steps I believe will help you become a successful writer of business documents:

◆ **Step 1: Understand the Demand for Good Writing**—If we don't write effectively, we get poor results. The pace and intensity of business demand that we communicate briefly and clearly—and doing so is a learned skill that richly repays the effort we make.

◆ **Step 2: Know Where You're Taking Your Readers**—It's a lot easier to find your way when you know where you're going. Define the message you want to get across to your readers and then build a straight and solid bridge to lead them to your point.

◆ **Step 3: Be Explicit, Clear, and Concise**—Don't present your readers with a murky swamp of vague terms, jargon, buzzwords, and stuffy phrases. Be precise and brief.

◆ **Step 4: Grab Your Readers' Attention**—Start with what's most important, unleash active verb power, and push readers' buttons.

◆ **Step 5: Write with Rhythm to Hold Your Readers**—When there is a smooth flow to your words and sentences, with good transitions to unify ideas, your reader will move easily through your message.

◆ **Step 6: Organize to Help Your Readers Understand**—Following the organizing method that's most suitable for each document you create will help your readers grasp the point you're making. Arranging ideas in a logical order, using introductory paragraphs, and separating sections with subheads will make your documents simple to follow and easy to understand.

◆ **Step 7: Choose a Tone That Produces Good Results**—Fit your language and your attitude to your readers—even when the readers are a diverse lot. This is a great way to empathize with them.

◆ **Step 8: Put Your Best Grammar on the Page**—Grammar is nothing more frightening than a set of simple rules. Grasp them, apply them, and bend some old ones.

◆ **Step 9: Edit, Rewrite, and Refine**—When you've written your document, take your readers' position. Edit the document for message clarity, organization, and mechanics. Refine your writing until your gut tells you it's ready for your readers.

◆ **Step 10: Master the Documents You Use Most Often**—If you become adept at writing the kinds of documents you produce every day—email messages, project proposals, customer letters, press releases, or slide presentations—you'll have much less stress and get better results from your efforts.

Enjoy the book, and use it to propel your writing to a higher level!

NOTES

Understand the Demand for Good Writing

OVERVIEW

Poor writing yields poor results

Why don't we like to write?

Effective writing can be learned

Good writing pays off

Today, business moves at such lightning speed that writers at every level need to deliver information instantly and accurately to a wide array of tough audiences. Top executives demand that your documents get to the bottom line immediately. Prospective clients need your proposal to explain precisely what separates your firm from competitors. And rank-and-file employees need written communication with clear direction and explicit instructions.

Poor Writing Yields Poor Results

With the electronic tools at our disposal today—computers, wireless PDAs, and mobile Internet-linked devices—just about everyone writes. Practically gone are the days when most professionals dictated letters to their secretaries. You'd think that with everyone constantly writing, we'd get better at it—but that's not happening.

Most experts believe the quality of writing on the job has worsened over the past 30 years. They point to the lack of clarity and to carelessly written emails that ignore basic spelling and punctuation rules. It's unfortunate that the business world has come to accept such poor writing.

A recent survey by Cohesive Knowledge Solutions (www.cohesive knowledge.com) revealed that working professionals spend 40 percent of their day on activities related to email—a third of which are considered wasted time. This translates into about 12 percent of the day or, financially extrapolated across the U.S. business landscape, more than $300 billion a year—wasted!

Getting people to send fewer emails is not necessarily the answer. One executive, responding to an Net Future Institute (NFI) Research survey, said the problem wasn't the number or frequency of emails; it was the inability of the writer to get to the point (*Hudson Valley Business Journal,* August 21, 2006).

If you're still not convinced about the impact of poor writing on productivity, consider these other reports:

◆ A third of workers in the nation's blue-chip companies write poorly, and businesses spend $3.1 billion annually on writing training (National Commission on Writing, panel established by the College Board, *New York Times,* Dec. 7, 2004).

◆ "Poorly written business communications waste time, drain productivity and cause errors" (*HR Magazine,* June 2006).

◆ Eighty-five percent of respondents said weak workplace communication wasted time, and 70 percent cited lost productivity, according to a survey by Communicare, Inc. (*HR Magazine,* April 2006).

Plus, in a publication by its Public Policy Council, the American Society for Training & Development (ASTD) reported that one of the biggest knowledge gaps was in writing skills.

Why Don't We Like to Write?

Writing is hard, and it's one of the least-favorite activities for most employees. For many of us, the problem goes all the way back to elementary school when writing was that most-dreaded assignment. Instead of encouraging us to be creative and experiment with words, many teachers stressed correctness—pointing out every grammar and spelling mistake. That was no fun! Nor, for most of us, was high school or college English. Flashback: That 1,000-word essay is due tomorrow and you're still 400 words short! Crank up some more sentences. Plug in some fancy new vocabulary words—that'll impress the teacher (even if you're not sure what they mean). Don't worry about rephrasing ideas already written. Just keep churning out those words until you reach that magic 1,000.

That's a terrible and stressful way to write. Because too many workers haven't let go of that high school essay syndrome and other habits formed years earlier, their writing continues to suffer. For them, the consequence is worse than a poor grade: people will lose interest and stop reading their documents.

I apologize now to all teachers of composition, grammar, and vocabulary—those topics serve critical roles in our language. As business writers, we need to follow the rules of grammar to make our documents clear and readable. And we risk embarrassing ourselves before supervisors, clients, and colleagues when we ignore basic grammar rules. So I appeal to all teachers, from elementary school through college: stress clarity and brevity, the qualities your students will need when they write in the business world.

Effective Writing Can Be Learned

Forget those long and drawn-out essays with complex words to demonstrate your command of the English language (or to show how well you faked it). The rules have changed since you were in school. With business text, your objective is not to impress the reader. Typically, it's to explain a situation, to suggest solutions to a problem, to offer instructions, or to recommend action. If you convey these points in a clear, concise, and organized fashion, you become an effective business writer.

This goal is well within your reach; just follow the steps in this book. Plus, pay more attention to documents from other writers, everyone from authors and journalists to top executives, middle managers, and support personnel. Notice what's well written and what's not, what's clear and what's confusing. As the reader, determine how effectively information is presented to you—a process that will help you generate documents that are clear, concise, and easily understood.

POINTER

Good writing helps demonstrate leadership skills.

Good Writing Pays Off

To a great extent, you are what you write in the corporate world. Co-workers, clients, vendors, and others may know you best by your writing, the most common means of business communication. Your words can convey anything from enthusiasm, intelligence, and empathy to laziness, selfishness, and ignorance.

Good writing helps demonstrate leadership skills. Company heads can shape the future of their organizations and inspire employees (see example 1.1). Senior-level supervisors can explain complex sales or management strategies. Mid-level managers can demonstrate or validate leadership abilities to subordinates and supervisors. And any employee who writes effectively will look better to the people who may play a role in determining his or her future with the company.

For example, a well-written document can show readers that

◆ you understand all aspects of the problem and can clearly convey them.

◆ you understand how the problem affects various people and departments.

◆ you've thought about potential solutions and can explain the options clearly.

◆ you know what steps different people should take and when they should take them.

Your Turn

1. Look through some recent emails from supervisors or executives at your company. Identify messages in which the language helped convey the writer's leadership skills.

EXAMPLE 1.1

Demonstrating Leadership Through Simple and Powerful Language

Here are excerpts from a CEO's letter to employees, shareholders, and clients, describing the positive results of a management style that some analysts considered controversial. In an effort to justify his management approach, the writer uses simple, compelling language and presents supporting data that illustrates the results of his leadership. The financial figures are stated simply (for example, *revenues rose 15 percent . . .*, *earnings increased 19 percent . . .*), so most employees can easily grasp them. Plus, phrases like *strongest results in the company's century-long history, energized by innovative e-commerce opportunities*, and *levels of performance and growth unprecedented in our company's history* drive home a simple and powerful message that credits all employees for the firm's success and inspires them to do even better.

To our employees, shareholders, and clients:

This last year was our finest, as 450,000 employees around the world helped us post the strongest results in the company's century-long history:

*   *Revenues rose 15 percent, to $89.8 billion, a record.*
*   *Earnings increased 19 percent, to $11.3 billion, the first time the company has broken the $10 billion mark in earnings from operations.*
*   *Per-share earnings rose 22 percent.*
*   *For the fourth consecutive year, our company was among Fortune magazine's most admired American enterprises.*
*   *Shareholders—including our active and retired employees who own $17 billion of company stock in their savings and pension plans—were rewarded with a 48 percent total return on each share of company stock.*

We begin this new year completely focused on the customer, energized by innovative e-commerce opportunities, and poised to move forward to levels of performance and growth unprecedented in our company's history.

We thank you for all your support in helping make this future so bright.

2. Examine a few recent emails from your subordinates, especially those that discussed a problem, justified a recent action, or suggested next steps. Decide whether your opinion of each person's capabilities was influenced by how clearly she or he explained the situation in writing.

The Next Step

Now that you understand how high-quality writing can enhance productivity and demonstrate leadership, your next step is to learn the most elemental skill of good writing—defining the message you want to convey. That's what we'll cover in Step 2: Know Where You're Taking Your Readers.

NOTES

Know Where You're Taking Your Readers

- Use questions to help you identify your message
- Jump-start your writing with a quick conversation, outlining, and free-writing
- Use a structured, step-by-step process for planning the document

Novelists, scriptwriters, and poets aren't the only ones who face writer's block. We business writers sometimes struggle to figure out what we're going to say and how we're going to say it. If you have a get-started system that works for you, feel free to skip this section. But if you spend too much time staring at a blank page or screen, check out the strategies below.

Start with a Few Simple Questions

Begin with what you know. Answer these questions to define your message:

1. What is the situation/problem/issue that is prompting you to write?
2. Why are you writing this document?
3. Who is going to read it?
4. What do your readers need to know?
5. What action do you want your readers to take?

To see how these questions help you begin writing, let's say that your company's travel costs are too high and the boss has demanded that costs be reduced. That's the answer to question 1—the problem that prompts you to write. The answer to question 2 is this: to inform workers in your division that travel costs must be lowered and to explain how the company plans to cut costs. The answer to question 3 (who are your readers?) is colleagues and others who report to you. There are several things that your readers need to know (question 4):

◆ Travel expenses rose 40 percent—$200,000—this year, compared with the same period last year.

◆ Our division must lower travel costs by at least $150,000 next year.

◆ Working with two other division heads, I've come up with three strategies to achieve this goal:

    a. videoconferencing sales meetings every other month

    b. booking plane tickets two months ahead of travel to take advantage of lower fares

    c. arranging for group rates at hotels specifically serving business travelers instead of at higher-priced properties.

◆ By November 15, we need to submit a written proposal for reducing travel expenses to management.

When your readers have taken in that information, you want them to do the following things (question 5):

◆ Review these strategies and give me your comments, changes, and additions by November 1 so I can submit the final proposal to management on time.

◆ Call me if you have any questions or if you'd like to meet in person to discuss the proposal.

By answering those five key questions, you've virtually drafted the entire document. I know it's not always that easy, especially with complex documents; but answer the questions in many cases and you're on your way.

Have a 60-Second Conversation with Yourself

No, I'm not asking you to act weird and talk to yourself out loud in public (well, not without a cell phone). But, like many people, you may find speaking to be much easier and more natural than writing. For one thing, you don't have to worry about punctuation and spelling when you talk. Just take those words flowing naturally from your lips to the keyboard.

Consider this scenario: You're about to start writing a memo to all senior management, including your boss, summarizing this morning's meeting about strategies for BC Industries, one of your firm's most important clients. This was a meeting your readers didn't attend. While staring at the blank screen, you get a frantic call from your boss.

"Listen," he says, "BC Industries wants me to be on a conference call in 60 seconds and I don't know what happened at this morning's meeting. Tell me now—what did we decide and what are the next steps?"

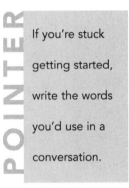

POINTER If you're stuck getting started, write the words you'd use in a conversation.

You're on the spot! But that's good because your supervisor's demand for the bottom line in 60 seconds forces you to get to the point and omit the unimportant details. Most likely, your thoughts would go immediately to the critical information you know he wants, and the words would flow naturally, something like this:

> *BC Industries had three system-level security breaches in the past six months. We suggest that BC invest $100,000 on a new software system that would prevent breaches at the application level. This purchase must be approved by October 1 to be fully operational by January 1.*

Well, there it is. Get text to flow naturally by approaching a document with the same urgency you'd feel if your reader was on the phone or standing beside your desk waiting for information.

EXAMPLE 2.1

Outline for a Plan to Outsource Training

Purpose: Suggest outsourcing training for customer service representatives (CSRs)

List simple, general categories:

I. Introduction: recommend outsourcing CSR training

II. Why we need it

III. Implementing the training

IV. Benefits of outsourcing the training

V. Cost

VI. Next steps

Expand categories with more details:

I. Introduction: recommend outsourcing CSR training

II. Why we need it

    A. Staff works inefficiently

    B. Too many customer complaints

    C. In-house training is not practical

III. Implementing the training

    A. Vendors (training firms) that would meet our needs

        1. Vendor A: pros and cons

        2. Vendor B: pros and cons

        3. Vendor C: pros and cons

    B. Setting objectives

    C. Scheduling

    D. Evaluation and follow-up

IV. Benefits of outsourcing the training

    A. CSRs working 15 percent more efficiently

    B. Better morale among CSRs

    C. More satisfied customers

V. Cost

    A. Vendor fees

    B. Payment to temporary workers to fill in for CSRs during training

    C. Other expenses

VI. Next steps

    A. Management approval

    B. Selecting a vendor

    C. Scheduling training

    D. Hiring temporary workers

Though most people reading what you write don't have to act on your information in 60 seconds, they're probably impatient. So have that imaginary conversation and put those spoken words onto paper or the screen. They form the core content of the document you'll write.

Develop an Outline for Longer, More Complex Documents

We're not breaking any new ground here. The traditional outline you learned somewhere between grade school and high school can still work well, especially for longer documents like proposals, plans, and reports. Start with general categories and then incorporate more specific ones. Example 2.1 shows the development of such an outline.

If roman numerals bring up unpleasant memories of dreaded assignments, use any combination of bullets and numerals that's clear to you. Remember, readers will only see your final document—not all the drafts you use to get there.

Free-Writing: Your Personal Brainstorm

Another method for getting started is called *free-writing* because it frees you from all those constraints of writing that can stifle your ability to crank out the right words—spelling, grammar, sentence structure, organization, and your own judgment. When you free-write on a topic, you just unleash your thoughts and get them down on paper as quickly as you can. What you write can be cut, organized, and better expressed later. What matters is that you dump out all your thoughts about the subject—and then feel good because you started!

Here's what free-writing might produce for a proposal to purchase new software:

Enough already. I'm so tired of hearing everyone complaining about the old software package. It's pretty well documented that it stinks. We gotta buy a new one. Tom said that 75% of the staff has complained about it. It's so very outdated that it has trouble with a basic program, there's absolutely no way we're gonna last even two more years with it before it blows up or something. Now we've got a shot a replacing it with a new software system that I think is kind of awesome in what it does . . . but like with every new thing in this place, any improvement we got resistance, so if I want it I gotta write this proposal that I'd rather not do, looking at everything it's a no-brainer. I've seen the studies from other firms who've used it, they all say the staff works 20% more efficiently, all say they can do functions they couldn't do before. And it wouldn't be that hard to get the implementation going, vendor says two weeks for the complete installation. I know how we'll divide up who does what. Joan (training manager) negotiates and works with the software vendor and will set the schedule for training. Bill (operations manager) knows this stuff well and will supervise the installation. This is all after we get George (chief financial officer) to get the funds approved. I hope he gives us the okay fast, we've gotta get this new system operational as soon as we can. Training will take some time but first we'll do group among everyone during the first 30 days, follow-up later that's individual. That'll happen in the second, third and fourth month. And the efficiency we get means freeing up the staff for other tasks that always get delayed now. There's no way the execs won't buy into this, but I shouldn't say that, they hate spending money unless you show all the facts.

POINTER

To free-write, just write down your thoughts on the topic.

Yes, that's a really rough draft, but it's a start.

To create order from the chaos of your free-written document, read it over and pick out the key points you need to communicate to readers. When put into a logical order, these points will form your outline. Using the free-written paragraph above, you might create the following outline:

    I. *Problem: existing software is bad*
       A. Outdated
       B. 75 percent of staff is complaining
       C. Can't do basic programs
       D. Won't meet future needs
    II. *Recommendation: buy new software package*
   III. *Benefits of new software package*
       A. Work 20 percent more efficiently
       B. Staff freed up for other tasks
       C. Can perform new functions
   IV. *Implementation*
       A. Installation
       B. Training
    V. *Delegation of responsibilities*
       A. George, CFO, approves funding
       B. Bill, operations manager, supervises installation
       C. Joan, training manager, works with vendor to
          create a training schedule.

Now you've got the framework from which to write sentences and paragraphs and arrange them in a logical sequence.

Use a More Structured Process

Some of you may feel more comfortable with a clearly defined step-by-step process that you follow from topic development to finished document. And some writing instructors (not me) believe that writers should follow the same process for virtually every thing they write. However you feel about that, a structured process can be an excellent tool when completing certain documents, especially the longer ones. If you want a process to follow, see the steps outlined in Tool 2.1. Modify the steps for your own style.

TOOL 2.1

A Structured Process for Preparing Your Document

1. Determine the purpose (what is the situation/problem/issue to be addressed and why are you writing the document?).

2. Analyze the audience.

3. Identify the key points to convey.

4. Identify the action you want readers to take.

5. Develop an outline.

6. Write the first draft.

7. Revise the first draft for message, organization, and mechanics.

8. Make the document visually appealing.

9. Proofread.

Your Turn

You can use many strategies to get started, including answering your own questions, using a simple outline, and free-writing. To practice different strategies, try these exercises:

1. Think of the next document you need to write. From your answers to the questions below, develop a simple outline.
   - ◆ Why are you writing this document?
   - ◆ Who is your audience?
   - ◆ What do your readers want to know?
   - ◆ What actions do you want your readers to take?

2. Read over a document you wrote within the past six months. Imagine that you had just 30 seconds to explain the key message to a colleague waiting on the phone. Come up with the words you'd use and say them aloud. See if you got to the point faster in your imaginary conversation than you did in your document.

3. Review the free-writing below and see if you could develop a practical outline from it. Remember that some points

should be omitted and that some ideas may be repeated at different points of the document.

Finally, yea, we're addressing a problem, 3 years what a pain in getting stuff in the hands of customers in the southwest states. So many of them have a fit when the products take as long as 2 weeks to arrive, can't have that no way. Everyone has their own idea about which city to open the new distribution center. Carl Miller says Phoenix is the Mecca of the southwest, I don't know where he gets that from, aside from thinking about going to some Phoenix Suns basketball games. I'm not saying Phoenix doesn't have pluses, like an able workforce, so we could easily fill the jobs, I don't know maybe 20 to 30. Whatever city it is, we've got to move on it, management wants it fully operational by July 1 of next year, 9 months from now. So decision time is upon us, by about start of Oct. Construction's gotta start no later than Feb. 1. At least weather is less of an issue in Phoenix, and with the other places in the southwest too. I say we hold a meeting with all the marketing and operations managers by this Friday, that's Oct. 5, discuss it, have everyone do their research and come back in three weeks so we can vote and get that decision done so we can move forward.

Ann Randolph will be at the meeting. She's been touting Santa Fe as this enchanted city, she's traveled there quite a bit. Actually, New Mexico is known as the land of enchantment, but who cares if they charge so much for rent, a helluva lot more than Phoenix for some unknown reason. Management wants good reasons for our decision, so we gotta go way beyond "enchantment." The best thing about Santa Fe is that they got the absolute perfect spot for the distribution center, I mean right off the highway and near a shopping center and if we ever have to visit, some outstanding pubs, but maybe I should leave this out of the next draft, I don't want anyone thinking my priorities aren't in the right place. Then you got good old Tucson, which has always had that weird quality to me. The guy in Chicago, I don't know him very well, Pete Marcus, thinks Tucson is hands-down the best place. Pros, the lowest rent and lowest construction costs. The cons, the location identified is hard to get to, 15 miles off the highway, on a treacherous 2-lane curvy hilly road.

The Next Step

Once you're comfortable getting started on a document, you need to write in a way that's easily understood, using as few words as possible. That's what we'll cover in Step 3: Be Explicit, Clear, and Concise.

NOTES

Be Explicit, Clear, and Concise

OVERVIEW

Avoid misunderstandings with precise details

Clear up confusion by changing word order

Avoid jargon, buzzwords, and repetition

Use fewer sentences to communicate your message

Despite our best intentions, our communication with others is often unclear. Popular culture often exploits our tendency toward miscommunication for its humor potential. For example, in "The George Burns and Gracie Allen Show," a classic 1950s sitcom, the often-ditzy Gracie Allen tries to tell a delivery guy where to deliver her new furniture. The conversation goes something like this:

> "Our house is right across from the Mortons' house," Gracie says.
> "What's the address?" the delivery man asks.
> "240 Grove Street," Gracie tells him. She hangs up and says to herself, "That's strange, I wonder why he asked for the Mortons' address."

That sure didn't work. If the delivery man had asked, "What is *your* address where the furniture will be delivered?" everything would have been clear. This type of silly miscommunication happens all the time, and it causes plenty of havoc in real life. If people would speak and write exactly what they mean, we could avoid so many problems and so much wasted time.

Be Explicit and Precise

Write text that's absolutely precise so it's understood the first time. Include all the pertinent details. Leave nothing to the reader's interpretation.

Here are two examples. Each imprecise version is followed by an explanation of what's wrong with it. A more clearly written version follows that explanation.

1. **Vague/imprecise:** *Cathy Jones is still waiting for your performance reviews. Her deadline for submitting them to human resources is around the end of November, and they require two weeks to review what you've recommended. So please turn them in on time.*

   From that paragraph, the reader can't tell when Cathy needs the performance reviews. Here's one way to make it more explicit: *Please submit your performance reviews to Cathy Jones by November 16. She needs two weeks to review your suggestions and must turn them in to human resources by November 30.*

2. **Unclear/imprecise:** *Shipping costs for the second quarter were 15 percent higher.*

   Were the shipping costs 15 percent higher than the first quarter that just ended, 15 percent higher than the second quarter last year, or 15 percent higher than all of last year? If you're using a comparative term (in this case, *higher*), you have to say what you're comparing it with. Here's one way to clarify the matter: *Shipping costs for the second quarter of this year were 15 percent higher than for the second quarter of last year.*

Sometimes we confuse a reader by the order in which we arrange our words. Consider these examples and the suggested improvements:

◆ **Confusing:** *Bob Reed told me October 1 that interest rates on the loan are 0.5 percent higher than anticipated, effective immediately, so please revise your figures.*

Does *effective immediately* refer to October 1 or to the date this message is sent? The reader can't tell from this sentence and won't know on what date to base the figures revision. Rearranging the words in one of these ways will clear up the confusion: (1) *Bob Reed told me that, effective October 1, interest rates on the loan are 0.5 percent higher than anticipated, so please revise your figures;* (2) *On October 1, Bob Reed told me that, effective today (October 15), interest rates on the loan are 0.5 percent higher than anticipated. Please revise your figures to reflect this increase.*

◆ **Confusing:** *I need to speak with Rick before his meeting today with the salesforce at 3:30.*

Do you need to speak with Rick at 3:30? Or is Rick's meeting at 3:30? Here are a couple of ways to clarify it: (1) *I need to speak with Rick today before his 3:30 meeting with the salesforce* or (2) *I need to speak with Rick today at 3:30, before his meeting with the salesforce.*

◆ **Confusing:** *This morning, I approached the management consultant with several good ideas.*

Who had the good ideas—you or the consultant? Here's a way to make that clear: *This morning, I approached the management consultant, who had several good ideas.*

Put Your Message in Context

Never assume your readers know the topic or context of what you're talking about in your message. At the moment when they're reading your message, their minds may be clogged with so many thoughts that they easily forget the issue/problem/project you're addressing. Don't worry about offending people who do know and recall the situation as soon as they see your name on the message. They'll appreciate the reminder, and your words will establish a context for messages that will be filed and referred to later. Here are two sample messages that lack context:

1. *I'm concerned that the project is taking too long, especially given the CEO's issues with the upcoming meeting.*

    Which project? How long is too long? What are the CEO's issues? What upcoming meeting, and when is it? Here's the way to write that so all the questions are answered: *I'm concerned that the renovation of the executive conference room should've been completed June 1—two weeks ago—especially given the CEO's desire to finish it before the board meeting on June 22, one week from today.*

2. *Paul, you made the same mistakes again, and we need to get this estimate done so we can submit for approval before it's too late. Please revise and get it to me in time.*

    Which mistakes? When did I do it the first time? When will *too late* be? This is better written: *Paul, your second-quarter estimate omitted travel expenses for the support staff, the same mistake you made on the first-quarter estimate. Please revise and submit to me by March 15.*

Use Simple Words, Not Stuffy Ones

Long sentences and pompous expressions won't impress your readers. Go simple every time.

◆ **Stuffy and wordy:** *Our determination of whether or not to retain the existing software system will conclude after the first-line managers have completed their evaluations.*

◆ **Plain English:** *We'll decide whether to keep the existing software system after the first-line managers complete their evaluations.*

◆ **Stuffy and wordy:** *You will be advised of my decision regarding whether our team will be able to meet the deadline that you requested as soon as I review the situation with my supervisor, after which I'll inform you of the outcome.*

◆ **Plain English:** *After I check with my supervisor, I'll tell you if our team can meet the deadline.*

Tool 3.1 suggests simple and direct replacements for some stuffy words and phrases.

Don't Catch the Buzz

Don't use pseudosophisticated words or techno-babble to show others how smart or business savvy you are. Your readers won't be impressed, and you may come across as insecure and uninformed about the subject. Although business buzzwords have become rather commonplace in office conversations, they're out of place in written communication.

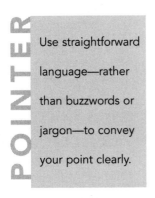

POINTER

Use straightforward language—rather than buzzwords or jargon—to convey your point clearly.

One buzzword I'm getting tired of is *leverage*. Primarily a financial term, it's defined as *the degree to which an investor or business is using borrowed money.* But today *leverage* is overused in place of simpler words to describe various nonfinancial situations. See these two examples:

1. *The company will **leverage** its well-established distribution system to create service programs for large regional operators.*

   There's nothing about borrowed money in that statement. Here's a simpler way of saying it: *The company will **use** its well-established distribution system to create service programs for large regional operators.*

2. *We need to **leverage** our resources to extract maximum productivity.*

   Here's a better way to say that: *We need to **use** our resources to maximize productivity.*

In both sentences, *use* conveys the point more simply than does *leverage*.

TOOL 3.1

Stuffy vs. Straightforward Words and Phrases

Stuffy	Straightforward
abbreviate	shorten
accordingly	so
acquaint yourself with	learn
advantageous	helpful
ascertain	determine, find out
as per your request	as requested
assumption	belief
at the present time	now
cognizant of	aware of
commence/inaugurate/originate	begin, start
consummate	close
conversant with	familiar with
due to the fact that	because
encounter (verb)	meet
endeavor (verb)	try
evident	clear
furnish	provide
inasmuch as	because
in lieu of	instead of
in regard to	about
in the event that	if
in the neighborhood of	about, roughly, approximately
of considerable magnitude	large
on the occasion of	when
peruse	review, study
precipitated	caused
predicated on	based on
prior to	before
pursuant to	according to
subsequent to	after
transmit	send
utilize	use

Let's look at some other buzzwords you should avoid:

- ◆ **Buzz:** *To increase productivity, the shipping department should **interface** with purchasing managers.*
- ◆ **Better:** *To increase productivity, the shipping department should **work with** purchasing managers.*
- ◆ **Buzz:** *We need to **incent** the salesforce to generate leads.*
- ◆ **Better:** *We need to **motivate** the salesforce to generate leads.*

Also stay away from industry jargon, especially when the audience is outside your industry. Want more buzzwords? See tool 3.2.

Don't let anyone tell you that straightforward language is too simplistic for the business world. Simplicity is the most powerful way to communicate.

State Your Points Positively

It's easier for readers to grasp what is or what should be rather than what's not or what shouldn't be. Here's an example of a statement with two negatives:

> *The southwest division shouldn't eliminate incentives for the salesforce.*

TOOL 3.2

Buzzwords vs. Simple Words

Buzz	Simple
actualize	produce, make happen, achieve
deliverables	objectives
interface with	meet with, work with
leverage (nonfinancial use)	use, take advantage of
discuss offline	discuss at another time
partnering	working with
take-aways from the meeting	next steps, action plans, or handouts

Do you see both of the negatives? *Shouldn't* is one; *eliminate* is the other. When the sentence is rewritten in a positive way, the meaning is immediately clear and instructive:

> *The southwest division should continue using incentives for the salesforce.*

Similarly, write what there's more of instead of what there's less of.

◆ **What's less:** *Regional managers pay much less attention to customer service than they pay to sales figures.*

◆ **What's more:** *Regional managers pay much more attention to sales figures than they pay to customer service.*

Drop Unnecessary Words

Thomas Jefferson, in his day a fine writer, understood the importance of being concise. He said, "The most valuable of all talents is that of never using two words when one will do."

It may sound like a tiny matter—one word or two—but over an entire document, useless words add up and waste readers' time. If you cut in half the number of words in your document, you help the reader grasp your message more quickly and save time for the other million things that must be done.

To make every word count, start by eliminating unnecessary or repetitious phrases that add nothing to the message. Here are some examples:

◆ **Overstuffed:** *It has come to my attention that the purchasing department doesn't track every invoice, which complicates budgeting.*

◆ **Lean:** *The purchasing department doesn't track every invoice, which complicates budgeting.*

◆ **Overstuffed:** *I thought you might like to know that more than 30 percent of the support staff will be taking vacations next week.*

- **Lean:** *More than 30 percent of the support staff will be taking vacations next week.*
- **Overstuffed:** *Let me start by thanking all the account executives who contributed to our team's success.*
- **Lean:** *Thanks to all the account executives who contributed to our team's success.*

There are many more unnecessary words and phrases that you may be tempted to use. Tool 3.3 lists some repetitious and meaningless phrases, and gives you lean alternatives. Remember, if it doesn't add meaning, nix it!

TOOL 3.3

Repetitious vs. Concise Terms

Repetitious	Concise
advance warning	warning
completely filled	filled
during the course of	during
for the month of May	for May
for the purpose of	for
honest opinion	opinion
important essentials	essentials
in an effort to	to
in conjunction with	with
in two weeks' time	in two weeks
located on, located in	on, in
merge together	merge
my personal belief	my belief
on a daily basis	daily
separate into groups	separate
the fact of the matter is	in fact
3 p.m. in the afternoon	3 p.m.
whether or not	whether

Fewer words should produce fewer sentences. In these examples, there's no need to write two sentences where one will do:

◆ **Two sentences and too many words:** *I read the budget report. I felt it was well organized, but, to me, it was overly optimistic about anticipated revenues.*

◆ **One concise sentence:** *The budget report is well organized but overly optimistic about anticipated revenues.*

◆ **Two sentences and too many words:** *At the sales meeting I attended, several issues were talked about. These included the two most important ones, the new marketing materials and the lack of administrative support.*

◆ **One concise sentence:** *The two most important issues discussed at the sales meeting were the new marketing materials and the lack of administrative support.*

◆ **Two sentences and too many words:** *Our marketing should be targeted only to a narrow audience. It needs to be focused on past customers only and not be directed at other audiences.*

◆ **One concise sentence:** *Our marketing strategy should be targeted only to past customers.*

We dropped words and punctuation and we combined sentences without losing any of the meaning—in fact, the message came through much more clearly with fewer words and sentences. (We'll talk more about cutting in Step 9: Edit, Rewrite, and Refine.)

Writing precisely and concisely can dramatically reduce the number of sentences you need to get your point across. Here are a couple examples of deep chopping:

◆ **Five sentences:** *The fourth-quarter report is a bit incomplete. This document needs more information on budgets. We need to know the amounts of money spent in the fourth quarters of the previous two years and how all those amounts compare with one another. So please make the necessary changes to this report. I do think it was well written, albeit without this key data.*

◆ **One sentence:** *Please revise the fourth-quarter report, which was well written but omitted comparable budget information from the past two years.*

When you've cut five sentences to one without chopping out any necessary detail, you're getting to the point fast—just what the reader wants. In this example, the impact is even more dramatic:

◆ **Wordy:** *I know customer service training is critical. The problem is that I'm not sure about the training you suggested that will occur on March 15. For my team, we need to address technical skills, its biggest problem. In the past, it's sometimes, but not always, included. My decision to enroll my team in this training is contingent upon the inclusion of this technical skills component. I'd appreciate if you could let me know either way. Then I'll make my decision, which also will be based on whether Sue's team will be able to cover our duties adequately on the phone on the day of the training.*

◆ **Concise:** *I'll enroll my team in the March 15 training if technical skills will be covered and if Sue's team can cover our phone duties that day.*

The difference: one sentence with 26 words vs. seven sentences with 106 words. And a statement that's so much easier to understand. That's some serious and successful cutting!

Your Turn

By writing in clear, straightforward language, you help others read faster without getting confused. Try the exercises below.

1. Replace the stuffy language shown in bold with straightforward text:

   a. *Larry was disappointed **due to the fact that** his boss never recognized his hard work.*

   b. ***As per our conversation,** your team needs to work smarter.*

2. Replace the buzzwords in bold with straightforward language:

   a. *If you disagree with Steve during our meeting, don't say anything. We'll discuss it **offline.***

   b. *This year, the boss wants us to work harder on our goals so we can **actualize** them.*

3. Rewrite this sentence so it's positive rather than negative: *The company shouldn't discontinue the vacation policy that's worked so well for 30 years.*

4. Delete unnecessary words in this sentence: *It has come to my attention that the northeast division is understaffed and is falling behind on production.*

5. Combine these three sentences into one, without losing any of the necessary detail: *Paul Jones called. He discussed several issues that need to be addressed. One was the lack of cooperation among the support staff.*

The Next Step

Writing clearly and concisely isn't always enough to get the attention of impatient readers. You need to hook them with compelling text. That's what we'll cover in the fourth step to successful business writing. That's what we'll cover in Step 4: Grab Your Readers' Attention.

NOTES

Grab Your Readers' Attention

STEP 4

OVERVIEW

> Compete for attention by getting right to the point
>
> Enliven text with active verbs and compelling language
>
> Direct your message to your readers' trigger points

We're always vying for readers' attention and pushing our ideas to be read in a business environment where employees at all levels are inundated with information. On a typical business day, the average worker is exposed to more than 3,000 marketing messages. These include newspaper ads, radio/TV commercials, billboards, transit ads, emails promoting business services, office posters pushing company activities, intranet ads, and much more.

Communication theorists call this *information overload,* a term I first heard as a college student in the 1970s. If there was overload 30 years ago, think how it's exploded now that the typical worker has a mobile phone, a PDA, and whatever the next new "must-have" communication tool is.

Most employees today are impatient and don't want to slog through several paragraphs before figuring out what you're trying to say. They want text that's explicit and concise, with a clear action step. In other words, they want you to *get to the point* immediately.

To connect with distracted employees, write documents that break through the clutter. In many cases, the quality of your document and how quickly you get to the point will determine how soon it's read—in fact, if it's read at all. For an example of an attention grabber, see example 4.1.

EXAMPLE 4.1

Getting a Prospect's Attention

Getting executives to pay attention to your letter or email is a challenge, given the amount of information they're deluged with every day. The following email, written to a principal in a public relations agency, led to a meeting with that firm. The first sentence addresses a critical trigger point for a typical PR executive—namely, that substandard PR writing hurts productivity. Then the three bulleted statements focus on other trigger points: sparking media interest, breaking through clutter, and generating favorable publicity.

Dear Mr. Lewis,

Even some of the top PR pros today don't write as well as they should—and that can hurt productivity. If this is the case at ABC Agency, I can help. I'm a 20-year PR veteran, corporate writing instructor, and professor. Having spoken recently on "Breakthrough Writing for PR Professionals" at the PR Institute, I know I can enhance the quality of your agency in the following ways:

- *As a PR writing instructor, I can teach your staff to write more concisely, to convey news value in just a few words, and to write copy that sparks media interest.*
- *As an award-winning PR writer, I can get those releases, pitch letters, news articles, and new business proposals to break through the clutter.*
- *As a PR strategist, I can give your clients the edge over their competitors by crafting innovative story angles that generate favorable publicity before their target audiences.*

To learn more,

- *see my résumé (attached)*
- *see the articles I've written on PR strategies and on the importance of good writing (attached)*
- *see my website for an outline of my corporate writing instruction (http://www.sgwriting.com/).*

Please call me at 555.782.2419 if you would like to discuss possibilities.

Sincerely,

Start with the Most Important Point

As we've seen in examples in earlier steps, writing clear and concise text means getting to the point right away. This skill is second nature for journalists because they need to capture readers' attention in the first paragraph of a news report. (Newspaper editors fitting copy on a page cut from the bottom, so the point of the story had better be at the top.) Having been trained as a journalist, I believe that starting with a lead—the point that's most critical—and following the lead with the other information in descending order of importance is the best way to hook readers. In journalism, this method is known as the "inverted pyramid."

Example 4.2 presents the titles and opening paragraphs for what could be online articles on a typical news website, where writers vie for readers by conveying the gist of their stories in one or two sentences. Readers who want to learn more click through to the full article; those who don't care to know more about the topic still understand the essence of the story.

You can use the same strategy with your business documents. State the heart of your message in the first couple of sentences. If

EXAMPLE 4.2

News Story Opening Paragraphs That Grab Attention

Barefoot Runners Gain with Pain

A growing number of female marathoners are braving painful blisters while transitioning to barefoot running, a move that's improving their times and strengthening their foot muscles.

No-Fax List Threatens Kansas Firms' Success

Many small businesses in Kansas are generating record sales by turning to an old technology—faxing—but the state's no-fax lists may quickly halt their success.

you don't, you may wander through a lot of introductory explanation and appear indecisive. See the example below.

- ◆ **Indecisive:** *Due to the systemwide failure, the difficulty in explaining the new procedures, and unexpected and sudden sick days, it is likely that we will deliver the XY project three to four days late.*

- ◆ **Decisive and to the point:** *The XY project will be delivered on September 15, four days late.* You can fill in the reasons why in the second sentence, if the reader needs to know.

You can also show you're in control—and demonstrate leadership qualities—by approaching the message from a problem-solution–next step perspective. Here's an example:

- ◆ **Too much introduction:** *It is my understanding that revenues showed a decline of 12 percent in the three quarters just past. We should do and need to do better. That means we need ideas that will produce an increase in sales. What I would recommend is the emailing of gift certificates worth $50 in value to all prospects. If successful, this effort could result in a rise in sales of 15 percent during the next quarter. For us to proceed, approval from Sue Ross is essential. If you could send her an email detailing the cost estimate of this initiative fairly soon, it would be appreciated. Then we could begin the project toward the beginning of May and see how well this marketing idea will work.*

- ◆ **Problem–solution–next step approach:**
    1. **Problem:** *12 percent decline in revenues for the past three quarters.*
    2. **Solution:** *emailing $50 gift certificates to all prospects, potentially boosting sales by 15 percent next quarter.*
    3. **Next step:** *email cost estimate to Sue Ross by April 15 so she can approve and we can begin by May 1.*

After you've listed those three points, put them into clear sentences:

Given the 12 percent decline in revenues for the past three quarters, I suggest emailing $50 gift certificates to all *prospects—which could boost sales by 15 percent next quarter. Please email Sue Ross a cost estimate by April 15 so she can approve the expenditure and we can begin by May 1.*

By writing according to that simple three-point outline, I chopped the number of sentences from seven to two, with less than half the number of words. To achieve this cut, I also eliminated these unnecessary phrases:

◆ *I understand that*

◆ *This means*

◆ *It would be appreciated.*

Here's another example:

I went through the report of July 15, which was just given to me. This report discusses the issue of mistakes made in bookkeeping. We find that these mistakes are up an average of 20 percent over the first six months of this year. The increase has been calculated from the same period, namely the first six months of last year.

POINTER

To hook readers, get to the point immediately.

It looks like we need some changes. Among the most important steps to correct this problem is giving 20 hours more training to the accounting team. I think you should notify the Learning and Development department to arrange to schedule a training session for this team in September and October.

Let's apply the problem–solution–next step approach to that wandering and wordy message:

1. **Problem:** *Bookkeeping mistakes rose 20 percent in first six months, according to July 15 report.*

2. **Solution:** *20 hours of additional training for the accounting team.*

3. **Next step:** *Instruct the Learning and Development department to schedule training for September and October.*

We can use virtually the same words to write one short paragraph:

> *Given the July 15 report revealing a 20 percent rise in bookkeeping errors, I suggest 20 hours of additional training for the accounting team. Please instruct the Learning and Development department to schedule training for September and October.*

That's direct and clear. And look at how much we cut from the original document:

- 38 words instead of 111
- two sentences instead of seven
- one paragraph instead of two
- five fewer phrases (all worthless):
  - *I went through the report*
  - *which was just given to me*
  - *the issue of*
  - *we find that these mistakes are*
  - *it looks like we need some changes.*

Unleash Verb Power

One of the best and simplest ways to enliven your text is to use strong verbs, the most powerful parts of speech in the English language. Wherever possible, write with active verbs instead of weak passive verbs and *verb-nouns* (also called hidden verbs). Let's look at some examples:

1. **Weak:** *Most workers **are in agreement** that shipping costs could be lowered.* This sentence uses the passive verb *are* with the verb-noun *agreement*.
   Strong: *Most workers **agree** that shipping costs could be lowered.* In this rewritten sentence, the active verb *agree* replaces the passive verb *are* and the verb-noun *agreement*.
2. **Weak:** *They are all **of the opinion** that monthly meetings can boost morale.* Here the passive verb *of* combines with verb-noun *opinion*.
   Strong: *They all **believe** that monthly meetings can boost morale.* The active verb is *believe*.

3. **Weak:** *New hires need to* **have an understanding of** *benefits after two months on the job.* The passive verb *have* joins the verb-noun *understanding.*

   Strong: *New hires need to* **understand** *their benefits after two months on the job.* The active verb is *understand.*

4. **Weak:** *Please take the account coordinators' suggestions under* **consideration.** Here the verb-noun is *consideration.*

   Strong: *Please* **consider** *the account coordinators' suggestions.* The active verb is *consider.*

5. **Weak:** *All regional managers need to* **perform an analysis** *of sales trends.* The verb phrase *perform an analysis* contains the verb-noun *analysis.*

   Strong: *All regional managers need to* **analyze** *sales trends.* The active verb is *analyze.*

POINTER

Use active verbs to pump up the energy in your text.

If those examples seem overly simple, that's because they are. Replacing weak verbs and verb-nouns with active verbs produces simple sentence structures that communicate the message clearly and in a more compelling way. And it *is* simple to do. It requires only that you look closely at what you've written and pump up the energy with straightforward action words. Tool 4.1 will help you identify verbs hidden in nouns and replace them with active verbs.

Enliven Dull Business Copy with Compelling Language

Let's face it: Most of what we write at work isn't thrilling—unless budget analyses, management reviews, and meeting reports excite you. Most of us would rather read the beautifully descriptive language of a novel, biography, or poem than the dry-as-toast verbiage of business writing. We can't use flowery words to enliven business text. Don't try recapping a meeting by writing that the CFO wore an *exquisite red paisley tie that complemented his finely tailored, single-breasted black suit* or that the *glistening sun lit the pudgy*

TOOL 4.1

Turn Hidden Verbs into Active Verbs

Verbs Hidden in Nouns	Active Verbs
are in agreement	agree
conduct a study	study
give a presentation	present
give a promotion	promote
give a recommendation	recommend
give a response	respond
give permission	permit
has a preference for	prefers
has a tendency to	tends to
has the ability to	can
have an understanding of	understand
it is her expectation	she expects
make a choice	choose
make a decision	decide
make an announcement	announce
make changes to	change
make modifications to	modify
make reductions to	reduce
perform an analysis	analyze
provide a summary of	summarize
take action	act
take into consideration	consider

cheeks of the account manager. Save that for your personal correspondence.

In the business world, you write more often about a situation than about a tangible object so it's difficult to be descriptive. But you can make text come alive, not with flowery or stuffy words but with compelling language that engages the reader. Here are a couple of examples that use lively words to express the energy of the information as well as the details of it:

- *The CEO fired up the salesforce at today's meeting, challenging it to uncover prospects' hot buttons and probe its long-term goals.*

- *In 20 years on the account service team, Jill Blass continually has exceeded clients' expectations, while training thousands of entry-level employees and developing innovative work flows that boosted efficiency by as much as 30 percent.*

Sometimes, changing a single word can make a huge difference. Here are two examples of sentences instantly improved by compelling words (in these cases, metaphors).

1. **Okay:** *The new five-year plan will **enable our firm to achieve** new heights.*
   More compelling: *The new five-year plan will **propel** our firm to new heights.*
2. **Okay:** *ABC Company's innovative marketing **is helping it achieve** unprecedented revenue growth.*
   More compelling: *ABC Company's innovative marketing is **fueling** unprecedented revenue growth.*

Want more examples? Just read a few newspaper and magazine articles and you'll find plenty of this powerful language.

Selecting words that enliven your text takes thought and practice—or a quick peek into an online thesaurus. Tool 4.2 offers some examples you'll find useful in drafting your business text.

Hit Readers' Trigger Points

If you know your readers, you probably know their hot buttons—what moves them to pay attention and take action. With CEOs, it may be profitability; with operations managers, it may be productivity; and

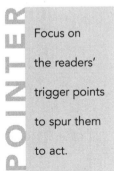

POINTER

Focus on the readers' trigger points to spur them to act.

TOOL 4.2

Bring Dull Business Language to Life

Dull Language	Compelling Language
Large amounts	Huge sums
Means the workforce is changing	Signals a shift in the workforce
Do better than competitors	Outshine competitors
Could result in more sales	Could spur sales
Help them find everything in the employee manual	Help them navigate the employee manual
Is a result of her 15 years of experience	Stems from her 15 years' experience
Objectives that will result in higher performance	Objectives to drive higher performance
Make up for the higher costs	Offset higher costs
Get customers interested in our other products	Get customers clamoring for our other products
We want employees to like using the new software	We want employees to embrace the new software
Introduce a new training initiative	Launch a new training initiative

Make background checks a requirement for new employees	Mandate background checks for new employees
Find a supplier that compares favorably with the current vendor	Find a supplier that rivals the current vendor
Outdated software could mean this project won't proceed as well as we'd like	Outdated software could stymie this project
It's our goal to significantly improve morale within six months	We're aiming to boost morale within six months
The CEO's new directive requires all employees to adhere to strict rules	The CEO's new directive imposes strict rules on all employees
As a result of the drop in consumer demand, sales haven't been as good lately	The drop in consumer demand has cooled sales
The CFO always finds a way to make our proposals look bad	The CFO always discredits our proposals

with HR directors, it may be morale. Here is some language that's likely to prompt the desired action from your reader:

- CEO: *If we open two new distribution centers, profits can climb by 8 percent.*
- Operations manager: *We need to hire 10 more people to achieve our productivity goals.*
- HR director: *To boost our sagging morale, I suggest holding two social events a quarter.*

Your Turn

Try these exercises to help you write compelling text more instinctively.

1. Replace the hidden verbs (shown in bold italic type) with active verbs. Change the word order in the sentence if necessary.

   - *We have two weeks to **make a decision on** whether to switch software vendors.*
   - *Because production **has had a drop** for the third consecutive quarter, we need to **conduct a study of** the entire cycle.*
   - *On Tuesday, the CFO will **make an announcement on** which of the proposed projects will be funded.*

2. Shrink this paragraph to one sentence that gets to the key point immediately:

   Changes have been observed in the workflow patterns at our southwest warehouse. Employees are handling far more tasks than they had previously as a result of the increase in orders. Considering this change, we should add to this warehouse staff by taking on eight more employees. It would be best if three of them had management experience.

The Next Step

Text that grabs your attention is not necessarily easy to read, especially with longer documents. Sentences need rhythm to carry the reader along. How to develop and use rhythm in business text is the topic of Step 5: Write with Rhythm to Hold Your Readers.

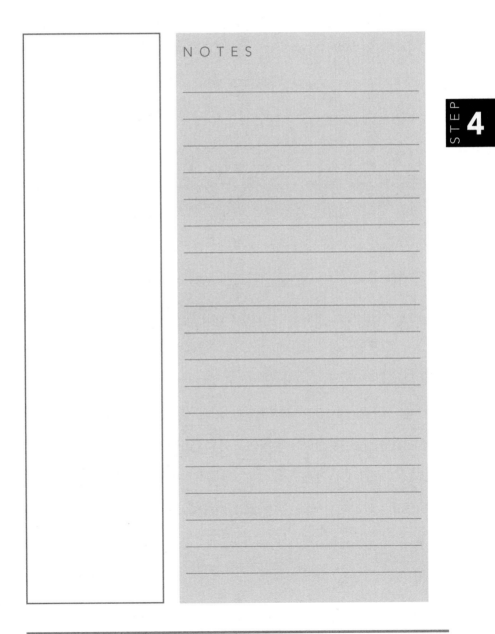

NOTES

STEP FIVE

Write with Rhythm to Hold Your Readers

Develop a feel for the rhythm of your words

Enhance flow by varying sentence openers, structure, and length

Use transitions to unify thoughts

Separate items with numbers or bullets

STEP 5

Like music, dance, and poetry, written words have a rhythm. We prefer songs with a pleasing beat and we prefer text with a pleasing rhythm. The right combination of words and sentences makes your text easier and far more enjoyable to read—and helps keep readers focused on your message.

Make Your Sentences Flow Rhythmically

To write with rhythm, create an easy-to-follow pattern from start to finish. That means beginning your sentences in different ways, varying their structure and length, making the components of your sentences and paragraphs balanced and parallel, keeping related ideas together, and using transition words and phrases to connect diverse ideas.

The first thing you have to do to improve the flow of your words is to identify the rhythm that appears naturally in your writing. To become familiar with your personal writing rhythm, read your first draft of any document out loud. Listen to the *sounds* and feel the *beat* of your words and sentences to sense how well they flow.

Vary Sentence Openers, Structure, and Length

Here's an example of a paragraph in which all the sentences begin in the same way:

> *During the second quarter, the absenteeism rate rose 18 percent, compared with the second quarter of last year. During this period, absenteeism was highest in the days immediately before holidays. At a time when keeping customers happy is critical, we need to reduce the number of unexcused absences. By developing a solution to this problem, our division will be able to achieve its productivity goals.*

Boring! Beginning each sentence with the same type of phrase produces an unpleasantly repetitive rhythm.

It's even more unpleasant when all the sentences begin with the same word—especially with "I":

> *I completed the external audit on March 10. I feel that VL Industries was not prepared to handle XD Technologies' shipping. I discovered that VL has no experience in the computer hardware industry and uses an archaic billing system. I think we need to conduct an online search for a vendor that has a track record in the computer hardware industry and an efficient billing system. I would be happy to answer any questions if you call.*

Varying the sentence openers for that paragraph can improve the flow a great deal:

> *In the external audit completed March 10, I found that VL Industries was not prepared to handle XD Tech-*

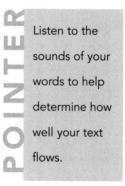

POINTER

Listen to the sounds of your words to help determine how well your text flows.

nologies' shipping. VL has no experience in the computer hardware industry and uses an archaic billing system. We should search online for a vendor that has a track record in the computer hardware industry and that uses an efficient billing system. Please call me if you have any questions.

That revised version covers all the same points that the rough draft included, but the reader isn't pounded with "I-I-I." The information flows from sentence to sentence and carries the reader along with it.

Making all your sentences the same length also produces an irritating rhythm that drains your reader's energy. Here's a paragraph comprising only short and choppy sentences. Read it out loud to feel its staccato beat:

The budget is due May 1. It needs to include estimated expenses for all divisions. Separate estimates are required for each division. This budget must include accurate training estimates. The last budget had inaccurate training expenses.

That sounds like a 21-gun salute! It needs sentences of varied lengths and different arrangements of words (something other than subject-verb-object), and it needs transition phrases to blend the separate points into a cohesive whole that draws in the reader.

Here's another example of a paragraph that's difficult to read because all the sentences are structurally identical—subject followed by verb—and all are short:

The annual meeting was held on January 15. Laura Smith is the president of our overseas division. She unveiled her marketing plan. She discussed several innovative strategies. The feedback on Laura's marketing strategies is due by May 25. We should meet to discuss various strategies. This should be scheduled for May 15 when I'm free.

An improved version of the paragraph has sentences that differ in structure and flow and that offer the reader a comfortable rhythm:

At the January 15 annual meeting, Laura Smith, president of our overseas division, unveiled her marketing plan. She outlined several innovative strategies. Because we need to submit feedback on her plan by May 25, let's meet to discuss it on May 15.

In the second version, I combined six short and choppy sentences to form three sentences. The first and third sentence use prepositional phrases: *at the January 15 annual meeting* and *because we need to submit feedback on her plan by May 25*. Between those sentences is a shorter sentence that varies the tempo.

It's not only a string of short sentences that's distracting for the reader. A paragraph composed of same-structure long sentences will be equally difficult to read:

After three months of observation, we have found that most first-line managers lack critical supervisory skills. According to the report, we see that 75 percent of these managers didn't adequately handle subordinates' complaints. From the report, we find that 60 percent couldn't explain their subordinates' daily tasks. Given these results, we need to develop an appropriate training for these managers. With this said, we should schedule a meeting on November 15 to determine the best training program.

Each of those five sentences begins with a prepositional phrase—yawn. Let's see what variety will do to improve the readability and interest:

After three months of observation, we have found that most first-line managers lack critical supervisory skills. Our report revealed that 75 percent of these managers didn't adequately handle subordinates' complaints and that 60 percent couldn't explain their subordinates' daily tasks. We need to develop an appropriate training for these managers, so let's meet on November 15 to discuss some options.

I kept the first sentence, but combined the next two ideas (the two statistics) into one sentence. Then I closed with a specific call to action. Better flow leads the reader to your desired action.

So you may be wondering which sentences are better—short ones or long ones. Some writing instructors believe that shorter sentences are easier to read. In some instances, short sentences are more effective—for example, when you want to convey urgency:

The client is livid! Nobody has returned his call for three days. We won't survive with this type of service. Call him in the next 10 minutes.

But too many consecutive short sentences can feel choppy and disjointed, as we've seen above. Longer sentences let you convey more information right away, and they let you combine data to reveal similarities or differences—but they can lose your reader along the way. Craft your sentences on the basis of your own style, the message you're conveying, and the tone you want to set. And be sure to use both long and short sentences where possible.

Let's look at a paragraph that has a varied and pleasantly rhythmic pattern of words and sentences:

In five years as a customer service specialist, Mark has handled product inquiries efficiently, written comprehensive monthly reports, and trained hundreds of entry-level customer service representatives. He's a true asset to our division. Plus, everyone on the team likes Mark and seeks his advice on many issues. Given Mark's consistently high performance, I recommend promoting him to senior account supervisor.

That paragraph, taken from a performance review, has long and short sentences, a variety of structures, and transition words and phrases that move the reader smoothly from point to point.

Write Balanced and Parallel Sentences

Some repetition can be effective. For example, using two clauses with similar structure or repeating words creates symmetry and a pleasing rhythm. This balance makes a sentence more readable. Consider these examples:

◆ *We prefer songs with a pleasing beat, and we prefer text with a pleasing rhythm.*

◆ *Our firm won't achieve its sales goals without investing $2 million in marketing, and it won't invest in marketing without clarifying the objectives.*

You also can use a balanced, consistent structure with two consecutive sentences, again creating that natural bridge from one thought to the next:

After our first meeting, the company to be considered for acquisition appeared to be on solid financial ground. After our second meeting, however, the company appeared to have several gaps in its accounting methods.

The components of a sentence are considered parallel when the same word forms are used or when certain words or phrases are repeated, usually in a sequence. Here's an example:

◆ **Not parallel:** *All division heads must pay more attention to improving productivity, expense reduction, and addressing customers' needs.*

In that example, the three things to which the division heads must pay more attention are not stated in a parallel manner: *improving* and *addressing* are special word forms called "present participles"—they're words formed by adding "-ing" to verbs. The second item in the list (*expense reduction*) isn't a present participle word form, so the list is not parallel. When you see the error, it's an easy problem to fix:

◆ **Parallel:** *All division heads must pay more attention to **improving** productivity, **reducing** expenses, and **addressing** customers' needs.*

Changing the noun phrase *expense reduction* to the present participle *reducing expenses* makes all three items parallel.

Don't Interrupt Sentence Flow

If the main idea of your sentence is interrupted by a divergent thought, readers may get confused. In the first sentence below, the prepositional phrase *at yesterday's meeting* knocks the reader's attention off the writer's point:

> *The accounting department found several discrepancies in our budget, at yesterday's meeting, which could short-circuit the entire project.*

The writer wants to tell the reader when the discrepancies were discovered, but putting that information in the middle of the sentence may derail the reader. If that information is placed at the start of the sentence to give the message context, however, the reader's attention remains on the writer's key point—discrepancies exist that could disrupt the project:

> *At yesterday's meeting, the accounting department found several discrepancies in our budget that could short-circuit the entire project.*

When you've written the first draft of a message, or when you're organizing your thoughts before writing, decide what is primary and what is secondary information. Then craft your sentences in a way that presents the information smoothly.

Don't Put Unrelated Ideas in the Same Sentence

This guideline needs no explanation. See how the unrelated ideas (set in boldface) take the reader off track in the following examples:

- *We need to recruit more experienced customer service specialists for the northwest division, **which just celebrated its fifth year at the new building.***
- *The creative team, **which has moved three floors up to a more quiet location,** doesn't understand the subtleties of our new product.*
- *XYZ Enterprises, **founded in 1935 at a Chicago warehouse,** complained about our technical support four times this month.*

If the unrelated information is significant enough to include in your message, give it its own sentence, bullet point, or paragraph. Don't risk losing your readers' attention or confusing them.

Use Transitions to Unify Sentences, Paragraphs, and Sections of Your Document

To unify your text, use transitions to link sentences, paragraphs, and sections. Transition words and phrases—"connectors"—bring logic to your text, bridging one sentence with the next and one paragraph with the next. They include words and phrases that typically are used to connect thoughts (see tool 5.1) and words and phrases that provide natural connections when they're repeated throughout the document.

First, let's try some of the typical transition terms to see how they improve a choppy paragraph that's trying to convey one idea but doing it with unconnected sentences:

◆ **Choppy:** *You should try writing like you speak to write better. You can do it when you start your next document. You should imagine that your boss is phoning from the airport and has only one minute to find out what you're about to write. This type of demand would force you to be concise and immediately state the most important point. This is how you should approach every document. It's true that most people who read your text don't have to board planes in 60 seconds. They're just impatient.*

◆ **Unified and flowing:** *If you'd like to write as well as you speak, try this: Before starting your next document, imagine that your boss is phoning from the airport with only one minute to find out what you're about to write. With this type of demand, you're forced to be concise and immediately state the most important point—and that's how you should approach every document. Although most people who read*

TOOL 5.1

Words and Phrases Commonly Used as Transitions

Purpose	Word/Phrase
To contrast	although, but, conversely, except, however, on the other hand, otherwise, still, whereas
To indicate results	as a result, consequently, so, thus
To indicate time or sequence	after, before, during, finally, first, later, soon, subsequently, then, until
To introduce another point	also, besides, if, in addition, plus, with
To prove a point	because, for the same reason
To give an example	for example, for instance, in this case, such as

your text don't have to board planes in 60 seconds, they're still impatient.

By repeating certain words and phrases—"hook words"—you keep readers focused and remind them of your key messages. In the following paragraphs, taken from a service proposal, three key points recur throughout (they're set in bold type and accompanied by a bracketed number to help you connect them from paragraph to paragraph). Although these phrases aren't identical in each paragraph, they make the same points.

The ABC Association plays a critical role in the insurance industry and offers **outstanding value** [1] to its members—but many people don't know this. The association needs to convey this and related **critical messages** [2] to members, prospects, legislators, and other key audiences. These targeted groups must understand the **member benefits** [3] that are available.

*With its extensive experience working for the insurance industry, XYZ Marketing can craft the association's **key messages** [2] and help convey the **exceptional value** [1] that ABC Association offers.*

*Among the **member benefits** [3] we would highlight are the legislative initiatives, educational programs, job training, and networking.*

*By integrating tactics such as web marketing, e-newsletters, and broadcast faxes, we will deliver these **vital messages** [2] about the association's industry prominence and the many **benefits of membership** [3]. In the end, this will help build a powerful brand for an association that offers **superior value** [1] to its members.*

POINTER

Repeat key words and phrases to focus readers on your central messages.

Separate Items by Numbering or Bulleting Them

Most readers find it easier to understand enumerated information—for example, the three marketing objectives, the five keys to earning a promotion, the four action items. Here's a sample of text in which the writer has enumerated his points in paragraph form:

*The vice president outlined three keys to generating new leads. **First,** attend a networking meeting at least once a week. **Second,** call at least 30 prospects a day. And, **third,** ask each existing client to refer two prospects.*

Here's the same text with the enumerated points broken out into numbered items:

The vice president outlined three keys to generating new leads:

1. Attend a networking meeting at least once a week.

2. Call at least 30 prospects a day.

3. Ask each existing client to refer two prospects.

Be sure to use numbers when the sentence that introduces a list cites the number of items in the list (as above) or when you want to present items in priority or performance order, as in the following action plan:

Here are the next steps for moving the warehouse from Atlanta to Savannah:

1. *Inventory all Atlanta merchandise.*
2. *Pack merchandise in boxes.*
3. *Get clearance that Savannah is ready for shipment.*
4. *Ship all boxes to Savannah.*
5. *Inspect merchandise for damage on arrival in Savannah.*

When the number or order of items is not an issue, it's fine to use bullets:

There are several departments housed in the Santa Fe division:

◆ *accounting*
◆ *customer service*
◆ *marketing*
◆ *order fulfillment*

One caveat on the use of numbers and bullets: use them sparingly. As is true for exclamation points and for the use of italic, boldface, and underlined type, overuse of numbered and bulleted lists blunts their effectiveness and ruins the text. Choose wisely for greatest impact.

Your Turn

To develop your own writing rhythm, spend more time reading your words out loud to hear how well they flow. Pay more attention to documents written by others, including those of co-workers, journalists, and authors, to see how well the rhythm of their words is working. Try these exercises:

1. In a business document, newspaper, or magazine, find a paragraph in which you believe the text flows naturally. Analyze what the author has done to produce that flow

and consider adopting some of that style in your own writing.

2. Revise the order of ideas in this paragraph so the flow isn't interrupted by nonessential information:

> *We can double production in our European division, as Stan explained during the flight home yesterday, by shifting our marketing strategy and hiring a sales manager for our London office.*

3. To create a more balanced sentence, rewrite the bold-type clause to match the style of the first clause:

> *Our shipping department needs to improve its efficiency, **and the high absenteeism rate in our production department needs to be reduced.***

4. Rewrite this paragraph to vary its boring sentence structure:

> *Laura Stark is the new vice president of the Asian division. She discussed her marketing plan at the January 20 annual meeting. Laura also outlined several innovative strategies. She mentioned the cost and expected return-on-investment. I would like to meet with you before February 15. We can analyze Laura's plan and come up with additional suggestions.*

The Next Step

Writing sentences that flow with a pleasing rhythm makes it easier for readers to move through your document and understand what you're saying. To further help readers grasp information quickly in documents of varied length, you need to organize the content so it flows logically from start to finish. That's what I'll help you do in Step 6: Organize to Help Your Readers Understand.

Organize to Help Your Readers Understand

Well-written sentences and paragraphs will not move readers to take action unless the document has a logical and coherent structure. In plain language, it needs to be well organized. Think of organizing text as the next step after ensuring that your words, phrases, and sentences flow with a pleasing rhythm.

You may want to start by training your mind to select and differentiate bits of information when you hear or read them. Before you begin writing your document, jot down the key ideas you need to get across. If you've started with a free-writing exercise, go through your first draft, pick out your key points, and move them around to create a logical order (see the outlines discussed in Step 2).

An organized document enhances clarity and encourages others to continue reading your text and to buy into your ideas. When you get used to applying these essential skills and techniques, you'll find that writing in an organized fashion will become a natural process.

STEP **6**

Most documents are
organized by one or more
of the following:

- order of importance
- time
- space
- comparison/contrast
- problem and solution
- existing categories

In this step, we're going to start with a discussion of the various methods of organizing a document. Then we'll address some of the organizing facets of a typical business document: the introduction, the key ideas/content, subheads, and topic sentences. We'll also discuss the use of executive summaries and ways to make your documents look inviting to the reader.

Choose Your Method of Organizing

Select an organizing method based on the type of document you're writing, the content you'll include in the document, and your personal preference. Among the most common ways of organizing are

- by order of importance
- by time
- by space
- by comparison/contrast
- by problem and solution
- by existing categories.

Organizing by Order of Importance

This approach is similar to the newswriter's inverted pyramid that starts with the most important information, followed by the next-most important material, and so on in descending order of significance. It helps ensure that those readers who are too impatient or lazy to read the entire document will get your key points.

Among the documents for which this method works are

- proposals
- project reports
- reports of problems that need to be handled right away
- research findings.

Example 6.1 illustrates this organizing approach for a proposal to purchase new software. The example shows the critical points somewhat fleshed out, but not written as they will be in the final document. You also could jot down general descriptions of the points to be covered—and these are shown in brackets after each specific point. That approach may be more useful if you're organizing your document before all of the data is collected.

Determining which point is most important is subjective. For the proposal used in example 6.1, you could argue that the old system's shortfalls are the most critical information and should be listed before the new software system. Only you know the specific details of your business environment and the personalities/roles of the readers, so use that information to prioritize the points in your document.

Organizing by Time

If your document deals with something that has just occurred or if it seeks suggestions or instructions for the future, let time dictate the organization.

EXAMPLE 6.1

Organizing by Order of Importance

The critical points in a proposal to purchase new software might be organized in this descending order of importance:

1. *New software system would save $250,000 in 12 months [primary benefit to be gained by the purchase].*

2. *Old system is too slow, has frequent shutdowns, and wastes operator time [primary problems the new software will solve].*

3. *New software received excellent reviews in industry magazines [industry recommendations supporting the new software package].*

4. *New system could be installed within two months [installation schedule].*

5. *Learning and development division could begin training immediately after installation [training schedule].*

This method works well for these and other types of documents:

- ◆ incident reports
- ◆ sales or trend reports
- ◆ instructions or action plans
- ◆ company history.

Here's how organizing by time could work in a report on sales for a calendar year:

- ◆ **First quarter:** *sluggish sales in 10 of 12 states*
- ◆ **Second quarter:** *telemarketing helps increase sales 10 percent nationwide*
- ◆ **Third quarter:** *outreach to five new districts boosts sales another 8 percent*
- ◆ **Fourth quarter:** *sales drop 5 percent below third-quarter sales after industry consolidation.*

With a longer time period to cover—say 50 years of a company's history—divide the years based on when events occurred. For example,

- ◆ *1950–58: Smith forms company and builds it to 100 people.*
- ◆ *1959–71: New owner expands to eight states.*
- ◆ *1972–90: Three new divisions form, revenues triple.*
- ◆ *1991–present: Merger with Jones Company propels unprecedented growth.*

For an action plan, the time-based categories would be the next steps in chronological order, with one or more paragraphs of detail after each numbered heading. This method of organizing is illustrated in example 6.2.

Organizing by Space

This method separates information based on different organization charts or geographic spaces: units, divisions, departments, regions, countries. For example, a customer service report might be arranged by service territories:

- ◆ **Mid-Atlantic:** *New software and training fuel 20 percent hike in customer satisfaction.*

EXAMPLE 6.2

Organizing an Action Plan by Time

If actions are to be taken in a particular order, organizing by time is the logical method to use. For a document outlining the steps a sales department will take in preparing for and capitalizing on the opportunities offered by an industry trade show, the action plan might be organized like this:

1. *Set sales goals.*

2. *Establish marketing plan.*

3. *Approve marketing messages.*

4. *Get budget approved.*

5. *Handle show logistics.*

6. *Attend show.*

7. *Follow up on leads.*

- ◆ *Midwest: Departure of division head leads to 10 percent decline in customer satisfaction.*
- ◆ *Northwest: Customer satisfaction is down 12 percent after team of inexperienced reps was hired.*
- ◆ *Southeast: Service holds steady for third quarter in a row.*

Organizing by Comparison/Contrast

This technique enables you to compare or contrast two or more topics. For example, a report comparing two divisions' performance in several categories might be organized like this:

- ◆ *Sales: southeast vs. central division*
- ◆ *Customer service: southeast vs. central division*
- ◆ *Operations: southeast vs. central division*
- ◆ *Morale: southeast vs. central division.*

As you can see by the example, that arrangement also creates a secondary organizing method (southeast division followed by central

STEP **6**

division), which is particularly useful if your topics are multilayered or complex.

Organizing by Problem and Solution

In its most simple form, this method presents the problem and then the solution. With multiple categories of problems and solutions, you first must decide the order for your categories. Then you easily can describe the problem and the solution in each category. Here's an example that's arranged by company holdings:

◆ *Texas property*
  ✦ *problem*
  ✦ *solution*
◆ *Louisiana property*
  ✦ *problem*
  ✦ *solution*
◆ *Oklahoma property*
  ✦ *problem*
  ✦ *solution.*

The problem–solution method can be modified to a strengths–challenges approach in a performance review. For example,

◆ **Overview:** *summary of employee's performance*
◆ **Technical skills:** *strengths and challenges*
◆ **Phone skills:** *strengths and challenges*
◆ **Working with team:** *strengths and challenges*
◆ **Individual work habits:** *strengths and challenges*
◆ **Recommendations:** *promotion, probation, more training, and more responsibilities.*

You also can organize a performance review this way:

◆ *Overview*
◆ *Strengths*
  ✦ *technical skills*
  ✦ *phone skills*
  ✦ *working with team*
  ✦ *personal work ethic*

- ◆ *Challenges*
  - ◆ *technical skills*
  - ◆ *phone skills*
  - ◆ *working with team*
  - ◆ *personal work ethic*
- ◆ *Recommendations.*

Organizing by Existing Categories

In some cases, the way you separate and organize information is dictated by natural categories. For example, in this report detailing the topics discussed at a marketing meeting, those topics are the organizing categories:

- ◆ *New slogan*
- ◆ *Print advertising*
- ◆ *Web marketing*
- ◆ *Direct mail.*

This category-based method also could be used for the different lines of coverage in an insurance company:

- ◆ *Liability*
- ◆ *Workers' compensation*
- ◆ *Auto*
- ◆ *Homeowners*
- ◆ *Marine.*

STEP 6

A Basic Method of Organizing

For some reports not defined by time, location, or preexisting categories, you may want to use a basic technique similar to the method many scientific reports employ:

- ◆ *Overview/situation analysis*
- ◆ *Findings*
- ◆ *Conclusion*
- ◆ *Next steps.*

Which Organizing Method Is Best for Your Document?

If you're not sure which way to organize your document, begin sorting out the ideas—a process that can help you select the best method or combination of methods. Here are some ways to find the key ideas for your document:

- ◆ Begin by writing out your ideas in one of these ways: (1) put each idea onto a sticky-note or index card; (2) write each idea on a notepad; (3) using a bulleted list, type each idea on the computer screen; (4) create a diagram with various circles, each with one idea inside.
- ◆ Review the ideas and see if you want to add, subtract, or modify any of them.
- ◆ Move the ideas around on the table or on your screen until you arrive at a logical order that will fit your organization's environment and readers.

In some documents, the content may demand that you use a combination of organizing approaches. For example, you may be outlining an existing problem, describing the recommended solution, and proposing a timeline or action plan for implementing the solution. It's OK to use more than one organizing approach in the same document, but do it carefully.

Write Introductory Paragraphs That Catch the Readers' Attention

The first paragraph of a business document must hook the readers, encouraging them to read more. Typically, an introductory paragraph conveys one or more of these items:

- ◆ purpose of the document
- ◆ situation/problem
- ◆ action required

STEP **6**

- benefits for the reader
- anticipated bottom line.

For example, here's an introductory paragraph that conveys the report's purpose and the action required:

Our account reps have been underappreciated since I was hired five years ago. This report will explain how management mistreats them, why their training is grossly inadequate, and what steps I recommend to correct this injustice.

Here's an opener that presents both the problem and the action required:

The annual conference is less than six months away and we still don't have budgets, sales goals, sponsorship packages, or travel plans. Each of you must give me this information for your division by February 1. Please follow the guidelines outlined below.

In the first few words, the following example tells the readers what they'll gain from the information in the document:

To help you and other managers work more efficiently, we've retained a management consulting firm specializing in time management. On March 1, we will start offering courses at no charge. This is a not-to-be-missed opportunity to increase your productivity. Below is the class schedule along with registration instructions.

Here's an introductory paragraph that clearly spells out how to reverse declining sales:

The 15 percent reduction in sales of building materials during the third quarter was due to the slowdown in new construction, colder-than-normal weather, and the lack of repeat sales among long-time customers. To boost sales going forward, we need to expand our market geographically, better train the salesforce, and increase direct mail spending by 10 percent.

STEP **6**

Separate Your Ideas

POINTER

Each paragraph or each section should address only one idea.

The biggest organizing mistake many business writers make is sprinkling information randomly throughout a document instead of dividing information into single-point paragraphs and sections. Ideas, whether self-generated or gathered from an outside source, seldom arrive in a way that makes perfect sense. Our minds don't always process information in an orderly manner the first time around—in our first draft. We have to make organizing decisions and apply those principles to our ideas, to the points we want to convey. If we take information from another source, such as a brochure, a website, or someone else's document, and don't subject it to our own method of organizing, we won't be presenting the message in the way we want to convey it.

Whatever the source of the material to be communicated to the reader, sort the information and separate it into "chunks." To do this, use one idea per paragraph or one idea per section. This chunking process makes it much easier for you to put the material in a logical order and much easier for the reader to digest your message.

Let's look at some examples. In the email below, the writer has scattered her ideas are all over the place. There's no organizing principle at work here!

Steve,

I enjoyed our breakfast meeting. Below is a review of the key points we discussed.

I'm excited about your aggressive sales goals for the next year. Plus, I agree that overall service to your customers needs to be improved.

We'll be able to talk about these issues during the 30-minute biweekly conference calls we'll set up, which we'll start on February 6. From our end, our biggest challenge to improve customer service is changing the attitudes of our phone reps, who don't give your customers the time

STEP 6

they need to resolve their issues. Starting January 15, all service reps will undergo a three-month training that will address attitudes and the need to understand your mission to exceed customers' expectations.

All customer issues should also be discussed on that first call, especially the report on customer surveys that have labeled our reps surly, rude, and curt. The calls also will enable your team leaders to get acquainted with our customer service managers. Again, our company is doing everything possible to help you achieve these goals cost effectively. You'll get a cost estimate by January 30, so we can move forward as soon as possible.

Please call or email me if you have any questions.

Regards,

Paula

If we reorganize that confusing message by separating the ideas into distinct paragraphs, we produce a much more readable email:

Steve,

I enjoyed our breakfast meeting. Below is a review of the key points we discussed.

First, I'm excited about your aggressive sales goals for the next year, and we're committed to helping you reach your goals. Doing so will take additional staffing on our end. I'll see that you get a cost estimate by January 30 so we can move forward as soon as possible. Our company is doing everything we can to help you achieve your goals cost effectively.

Second, we agree that service to your customers needs to be improved. This requires changing the attitudes of our phone reps, who don't give your customers the time they need to resolve their issues. In customer surveys, our reps have been labeled surly, rude, and curt. Starting January 15, all service reps will undergo a three-month training that will address attitudes and the need to achieve your mission of exceeding customers' expectations.

Third, the biweekly conference calls will be critical in addressing all service issues and will enable your team leaders to get acquainted with our customer service managers. We'll schedule 30-minute calls every other Wednesday at 8:30 a.m., starting February 6.

Please call or email me if you have any questions.

Regards,

Paula

In the revised version, each paragraph addresses a distinct issue, and that makes the information easier for the reader to manage.

Use Subheads to Highlight Each Concept

To further separate ideas and clue your readers to where you're going next, write subheads before each major section. Even in shorter documents written as email, subheads can enable readers to grasp your message faster. Plus, subheads eliminate one of the biggest obstacles to readability—the dreaded Blob of Text.

Take a minute to read the following paragraph:

I have several suggestions for marketing the new line of products over the course of the year. First, we should place full-page, four-color magazine ads for the entire year in the five most important trade publications, which are all monthlies. Cost: $100,000. Another suggestion is to place banner ads on the 10 key industry websites for the year, which would include two-way links. Cost: $20,000. Plus, we should also conduct four direct email campaigns, targeted to all who previously purchased our products or expressed interest in similar products online over the last three years. Cost: $30,000. Let's not forget traditional direct mail. We should send product flyers to existing customers of all product lines three times during the year. Cost: $50,000. And I'd recommend that we conduct five educational breakfast seminars on the entire product line. We would secure outside speakers and hold the events at upscale venues in the southeast region. Cost: $75,000. Let me know what you think of these ideas so we can move forward.

To the reader, that paragraph is a blob of black ink that goes on too long without a break—it's a turnoff. But simply adding subheads to separate the marketing suggestions makes a tremendous difference in appearance and in readability:

I have several suggestions for marketing the new line of products over the course of the year:

Magazine ads

Place full-page, four-color magazine ads to run all 12 months in the five most important trade publications. Cost: $100,000.

Banner ads

Place banner ads on the 10 key industry websites. The ads should include two-way links. Schedule them to run all year. Cost: $20,000.

Direct email

Conduct four direct email campaigns, targeted to everyone who previously purchased our products or expressed interest in similar products online over the past three years. Cost: $30,000.

Traditional direct mail

Three times a year, send product flyers to existing customers of all product lines. Cost: $50,000.

Educational seminars

Conduct five educational seminars on the entire product line. These should be breakfast events held at upscale venues in the southeast region. Outside speakers should be invited. Cost: $75,000.

Let me know what you think of these ideas so we can move forward.

With those subheads, the reader immediately sees the five suggestions and can choose which one to review first. If the reader is

Use subheads that are explicitly related to the topic to draw your readers in to your message.

already thinking about where to place banner ads, he can turn to that category first.

For certain documents, including those trying to convince readers to take action (like purchase your firm's products), use subheads that are explicit—that summarize the key points conveyed in that paragraph or section. These act like newspaper headlines that lure readers into your document. Let's compare the ordinary and explicit subheads used in a proposal for new security software (example 6.3). Whereas the subheads on the left offer a broad overview of the text to follow, the ones on the right specify the key message expressed in that section, enticing readers to learn more. For example, instead of the general subhead, "Key Benefit Number 1," the explicit subhead describes the benefit: "Prevents unauthorized copying of valuable data."

EXAMPLE 6.3

Ordinary vs. Explicit Subheads in a Proposal for Security Software

Ordinary Subhead	Explicit Subhead
Background/problem	Number of security breaches has tripled in 5 years
Objective	Need to safeguard intellectual property
Solution	Software provides security solution at operation and application levels
Key benefit #1	Prevents unauthorized copying of valuable data
Key benefit #2	Seamlessly integrates with document management systems
Key benefit #3	Supports all CAD and business programs
Next steps	Approve by April 1, install by May 1

STEP 6

Begin Sections and Paragraphs with Topic Sentences

Begin every section or new-subject paragraph with a topic sentence that tells readers where you're going. Going back to Paula's meeting recap with Steve (on pages 71–72), see how each topic sentence set the tone and established the context for the rest of the paragraph:

- *First, I'm excited about your aggressive sales goals for the next year, and we're committed to helping you reach your goals.*
- *Second, we agree that service to your customers needs to be improved.*
- *Third, the biweekly conference calls will be critical in addressing all service issues and will enable your team leaders to get acquainted with our customer service managers.*

Each paragraph continued with specific details related to the topic described in the first sentence.

Use Executive Summaries with Longer Documents

Have you ever worked your tail off on a lengthy document—like a 20-page report—and then wondered whether your supervisor read all of it? If he or she hasn't read most of what you've written, then you've wasted a lot of time and your supervisor may have missed your key points entirely. That's why you need to start any long document with an executive summary that briefly explains your key points. The goal of your summary is to give enough information to intrigue the reader to study the full report.

POINTER

For longer documents, write an executive summary that explains your key ideas in a few paragraphs.

Example 6.4 is an executive summary for a proposal to build membership in an association.

This executive summary includes only the most essential points of XYZ's communication

EXAMPLE 6.4

Executive Summary for a Proposal to Build Membership

The ABC Association plays a critical role in helping its members—electrical suppliers—grow their businesses, but many suppliers in the industry don't realize that. The association needs to position itself as the source for success in the electrical supply field, a message that should be delivered to members, prospects, and other key audiences.

XYZ, a communications firm with 10 years' experience in the electrical supply industry, can craft this message. We will explain how the association offers outstanding member value—through educational programs that improve management functions, networking events that generate new business leads, and a members-only website that provides vital industry news.

Our communication program will integrate tactics such as web marketing, print and e-newsletters, and broadcast faxes. In the end, ABC will build a powerful brand—as an association that electrical suppliers can rely on to help achieve their goals—and will be able to recruit more members.

program to build ABC Association's membership—describing the basic situation, what XYZ brings to the table, and the payoff for ABC.

- ◆ ABC Association needs to position itself as the source for business success among electrical suppliers.
- ◆ ABC needs to deliver this message to target audiences (members, prospects, legislators, and others).
- ◆ XYZ has 10 years of experience in the electrical supply industry and the expertise to craft messages about ABC's educational programs, its networking, and its members-only website.
- ◆ XYZ will integrate different tactics to build a powerful brand for ABC.

The full proposal elaborates on those points and addresses other points, including

- ◆ the background of ABC Association
- ◆ challenges that electrical suppliers face and why the suppliers need to belong to ABC Association

- ABC's need to recruit members and other objectives
- a further breakdown of the target audiences
- specifics on how ABC would be positioned as the source for business success in the electrical supply industry
- more detail on XYZ's experience, including its track record in the electrical supply field
- specifics on membership benefits, including the types of educational programs ABC offers, topics covered at ABC events, and examples of industry news available on the members-only website
- other membership benefits not mentioned in the executive summary
- details on how each membership benefit would be communicated to the target audiences
- specifics on different tactics, including the content and frequency of the newsletters, broadcast faxes, and other web marketing tools
- details on how the communication program would produce new members
- explanation of how other ABC objectives would be achieved
- a timeline for the communication program
- a budget.

From XYZ's perspective, all of those points are valuable in getting ABC Association to buy into the communication plan. But only the *most essential points* should be included in the executive summary—enough to show what sets XYZ's plan apart from competitors' plans.

Make Your Document Look Good

Making your document look good is a fairly simple way to add clarity and invite readership. An organized appearance is a strong support for organized thoughts. Here are some tips:
- Number the sections.
- Use short paragraphs (this goes with the strategy of presenting one idea per paragraph).

- Use bullets where appropriate—but remember that overuse can make your document visually displeasing.
- Set subheads apart with bold type, italics, underscores, all caps, or color.
- After a heading, insert a hard return instead of putting text on the same line.
- Skip lines between paragraphs or sections.
- Start a paragraph on a new page instead of breaking the paragraph from page to page.
- Use at least 1.5 spaces between lines in a paragraph.

Use some of those tips to create a visually appealing document. Example 6.5 shows how you can make an email message look good with headings, numerical categories, and further divisions with bullets. Notice that the first paragraph mentions the three numbered sections in that order.

For documents generated in Word, use a combination of bold and underscore. See example 6.6.

Your Turn

There are many ways to organize text, depending on the document, the situation, the reader, and your own preference. Try these exercises to hone your organizing skills:

1. Pick out the three main ideas expressed in the wordy and rambling message below. For each of the ideas, write an explicit subhead that will lure readers.

   I enjoyed our dinner meeting. I've been thinking about all the ideas discussed, so here's a review along with some ideas. For one, I'm excited about your expansion plans for next year. If this happens, we'll generate 35 percent more leads and generate $15 million more in revenues. Plus, I agree that we have a problem with customer service reps concerning their inefficient daily interaction with clients. Let's

EXAMPLE 6.5

A Visually Appealing Email

Lou,

It was a pleasure meeting you last Tuesday. I look forward to working with you on the leadership training program. Below, you'll find a review of the key points we discussed, a suggested course outline, and the next steps.

1. *KEY POINTS DISCUSSED*
   - *Program objective: Get midlevel managers to exhibit leadership skills*
   - *Estimated budget: $75,000*
   - *Timeframe: March 1 to June 1*
   - *Training hours per month: 50*

2. *SUGGESTED OUTLINE*
   - *Defining leadership*
   - *Evaluating leadership qualities*
   - *Cases studies in leadership*
   - *Importance of execution*
   - *Role play*
   - *Wrap-up*

3. *NEXT STEPS*
   - *Approve budget, timeframe, and outline*
   - *Determine enrolment*
   - *Reserve rooms and handle logistics*

Regards,

Susan

STEP 6

not forget about improving performance of the sales staff.

So many customers have complained about the attitudes of our phone reps. I've heard comments like "surly," "obnoxious," and "unsympathetic." We can't have that. I think we've got put all these reps into a two-day, in-house customer service training. Mary Logan, a long-time phone supervisor, can do this in the

EXAMPLE 6.6

A Visually Appealing Report

Overview

Last year's public relations program helped build visibility for key areas of PDQ Company, in the process positioning the firm as a more prominent industry player. As a result, the company has become a recognized media source, which has built credibility before key audiences.

Major 2007 Placements

- *Extensive pickup of six press release introducing new products*
- *Three company profiles in prominent trade magazines*
- *Speaker forums at two of the most important industry trade shows*

Placements Anticipated in First-Quarter 2008

- *Washington Post (early February)*
- *Wall Street Journal (late February)*
- *Business Week (late March or early April)*

Recommendations for Remainder of 2008

For the rest of 2008, we need to accelerate the proactive media relations program by moving into other media, including TV, radio, and the Internet. We'll suggest story angles centered on key industry trends and breaking news stories; and we'll prepare PDQ spokespeople to ensure that the company's critical messages are delivered.

next two months. It should start by October 1. That way, we can be ready for the holiday season.

The salespeople are not progressing like they're capable of. They're very resistant to change. One big example is that they're targeting only the top people at companies and forgetting about the IT directors who have plenty of influence on technology purchases. Let's call Frank Starks, who has sold to IT people for 25 years, and get him to speak at the next sales meeting to explain the keys to reaching this audience.

2. Write a topic sentence for the following poorly written paragraph. The sentence should frame the key message and replace the existing first sentence.

My meetings with each account coordinator indicated that the three new managers berate their subordinates in public, which is not acceptable. As a result, morale among account coordinators is way down since the new managers took over six months ago, and it has negatively affected production. Looking back, all three came to us with in-depth product knowledge—which is critical—but with limited management experience. We believed they would fit in from the start. They could still be effective with some high-level training. I suggest the M&O Associates' four-day management training, which stresses empathy for subordinates and better team performance.

The Next Step

An organized document promotes clarity and understanding, and it helps sell your ideas to your readers. Still, enticing others to take action often requires us to consider such factors as the specific situation and your relationship to the readers. That's discussed in Step 7: Choose a Tone That Produces Good Results.

NOTES

N O T E S

Choose a Tone That Produces Good Results

OVERVIEW

Guidelines for categorizing your readers and your relationship with them

Tips for writing to specific readers—supervisors, peers, subordinates, and customers

Helpful instructions for setting a tone that will satisfy everyone

Just as facial expressions, voice, and body language affect speech, the tone of your text can deliver different messages and evoke certain reader actions and feelings. Your language can convey anything from empathy and enthusiasm to indifference and disdain. You also can demonstrate leadership, convince a neutral reader to buy into your idea, or help turn a livid customer into a loyal one.

Know Your Readers

The more you know about who'll be reading your document, the better you can tailor your text to produce the desired results. There are two major ways to divide the categories of readers:

1. how they'll receive your message
2. what your relationship is with them

By anticipating how readers will receive your message (for example, open, indifferent, or hostile), you can better tailor your messages. Here are some strategies for writing to suit your readers' anticipated attitudes:

- **For readers who are open to your message, be natural and conversational:** For close colleagues or others you feel comfortable with, a warm and friendly tone works best. Here's an example:

    You and I know that customer service representatives can reduce the number of errors. All they need is the right training and some kudos from you, me, and the rest of the management team.

- **For readers who are indifferent to your message, be persuasive:** With readers who don't know you that well or who have no stake in whether your ideas are well received, you need to convince them to buy into your concept. This is especially true when writing to people with the power to spend the company's money. Here's an example:

    We should invest in this new software program because it will improve productivity by 15 percent and free the salesforce to generate more leads.

- **For readers who are hostile to your message, find common ground between your message and their needs:** To hold the attention of a hostile reader (like a division head annoyed with your team or a customer dissatisfied with the product), demonstrate that you understand she or he is upset and that you've developed a potential solution to the problem. Here's an example:

    I agree that my team's service has declined due to a lack of technical knowledge among our account reps. Starting tomorrow, all reps will attend a two-day training that will help them identify customers' technical needs and direct callers to the proper department more quickly.

Establishing your tone on the basis of your relationship to the reader also is an effective way to produce the desired results. Below

STEP 7

are some general rules to follow, depending on the existing relationship.

Writing to Supervisors

Effective communication with superiors can validate your abilities, including your leadership skills. By writing clear and concise documents, you can demonstrate the value you bring to the table.

Decide whether to use a formal or an informal style based on your supervisor's preferences and the way you typically interact with him or her. Always show respect. It also helps to know your boss's outside interests and whether he or she has a sense of humor. Plus, look at your supervisor's writing style and see what you could pick up and display in your correspondence with him or her.

POINTER

Write explicit text to convey your confidence to supervisors.

Your documents should convey an appreciation of what's important to supervisors and what motivates them—their trigger points. These might include goals for the company or the division, the pressures they face, or their budget constraints.

Here's a sample scenario in which you need to choose words carefully to establish the right tone: Your supervisor is unhappy with your team's drop in production during the first quarter. You attribute this drop to the laying off of two people in the fourth quarter of the previous year. The boss wants your explanation for the decline and your plan to bring production back up to last year's level. Your email should

1. convey that you understand why he's upset
2. remind him of the reduction in staff, without making it an excuse
3. exude confidence in your ability to increase production, despite the reduction in staff.

Here's how your letter might read:

Mr. Simmons,

I agree that production must improve to at least the level of last year—and we probably can do even better. The months following the layoffs of Carol and Stan have been challenging, but the team has begun to adapt to their loss and to work more efficiently.

I've developed a new lead-generation system that I believe will improve production over last year's level. Please review the details below. I'm excited about moving forward with this new system, assuming you approve it.

Thanks,

Laura

Let's review what parts of that document delivered the appropriate tone:

1. Conveys that you understand why the boss is upset: *I agree that production must improve to at least the level of last year—and we probably can do even better.*
2. Reminds him of the reduction in staff, without making it an excuse: *The months following the layoffs of Carol and Stan have been challenging.*
3. Exudes confidence in your ability to increase production, despite the reduction in staff: *I've developed a new lead-generation system that I believe will improve production over last year's level.*

Writing to Peers

Though the business environment is competitive, documents written to peers shouldn't reflect a me-first or an I'm-better-than-you attitude. Instead, they should convey that you're all part of the same company or team, committed to its success. For example, if you want to get buy-in from others for your idea, craft your message so you don't come across as the creative genius who everyone should follow. Below are the wrong and right approaches to such a situation:

My Great Idea

For six months, we've been racking our brains to figure out how to reduce costs for trade shows, especially the exorbitant shipping costs for the booth. Not any more. Through extensive research, I've found a way to produce a modular exhibit that weighs less than half of our existing booth. Shipping costs would be 35 percent less. This idea is a winner! Please review the details and email me your endorsement as soon as you can.

Whoa! Such boastful language, raising yourself above your peers, won't win you any allies. Here's a better approach:

Input wanted

In light of our challenge to reduce trade show shipping costs, I'd like you to consider this alternative: a modular exhibit that weighs less than half of our existing booth and would ship for 35 percent less. I'd love your feedback on this idea and any other suggestions you have for reducing shipping costs.

That message conveys the same information as the first one, but it does so in a collegial, respectful way. The writer isn't fawning or begging but merely addressing the reader peer to peer.

Writing to Subordinates

Your communication to those who report to you plays a critical role in building your relationship with them (and in building your career). Every email to subordinates is an opportunity to motivate, demonstrate support, and build morale.

As a manager or supervisor, you'll have many occasions to address mistakes that your subordinates have made. How you describe the situation and communicate your feelings and your wishes is set by the tone you take in your message. Here are two examples:

STEP **7**

1. **Negative, critical tone:** *I'm appalled by the number of payroll errors you've made on the ABC Industries account. This account is vital to us, and we will not tolerate such carelessness. Each of you **must** attend a meeting this Tuesday at 9 a.m. to review procedures so we can eliminate these errors! This is a mandatory meeting!*

2. **Productive tone:** *Several serious errors have been made on the payroll for ABC Industries, a vital account to us. Each of you needs to be more careful. We will meet this Tuesday at 9 a.m. to review procedures and develop methods to help eliminate errors.*

That first email will turn off most readers, many of whom will react with anger, guilt, or other negative emotions that probably will make them less productive (at least for that day) and less committed to solving the problem.

Let's look more closely at the issues of criticism and praise and at how to express them effectively in messages to subordinates.

Be Specific with Your Criticism

When you need to criticize employees who report to you, address specific mistakes they've made instead of broad personality traits they exhibit. (Such personality issues probably should be addressed in a face-to-face meeting.) Clearly define the next steps they should take to correct the problem.

Below are two versions of an email to a subordinate, criticizing his lack of attention to a customer:

1. **Vague criticism and recommendation:** *Ann Johnson of XYZ Industries is furious. You haven't been paying enough attention to her requests. We'll lose this client if you continue to be so indifferent! Your service skills must improve immediately.*

2. **Specific criticism and recommendation:** *Ann Johnson of XYZ Industries is upset that you haven't returned two calls over the past five days. She needs you to fix a software malfunction right away. Remember to always return her*

calls within 24 hours. XYZ is one of our best clients and we can't afford to lose them. I suggest that you call her immediately and meet with her early next week to listen to all of her concerns.

Temper Your Criticism When Necessary

In some cases, you want to point out a subordinate's mistake without coming across too negatively. This calls for a tempered message. Maybe you should label the error as one example of a departmentwide problem to which others are contributing as well. If appropriate, you can remind your reader that he or she is a valuable asset to the company, despite the mistake. Here's an example:

Stan,

I appreciate all of your high-caliber work on the BBQ Railways project over the past two months. It has freed my time for other critical projects.

But you need to be more careful with the monthly client memos. The April memo mistakenly reported that BBQ was two months behind in its payment. That mistake upset several of the firm's top executives.

I understand that these memos are copied and pasted from existing documents and that mistakes happen. In fact, many others on our team have made similar errors over the past six months. We need to put a stop to it. Next week, I will send an email reminding everyone to review memos more carefully and to be sure that two other people proofread text and figures before the documents are sent.

Again, keep up the good work, and be more careful with client memos.

Thanks,

Mike

STEP **7**

Give Both Broad and Specific Praise
When Merited

Although flattering others can elevate their self-esteem and boost their morale, it can backfire if it's perceived as insincere or patronizing. If you praise an employee every time she does something right with statements like, *Thanks for being a great team player* or *Wow, what a great job!* your message quickly will come across as phony and lose its impact. Then, when she achieves a feat that truly deserves a compliment, your kind words will seem disingenuous or be ignored entirely.

When a person's work calls for praise, you can include both a broad stroke on that person's value to the company and kudos for the particular efforts that have paid dividends. Here's an example of just such a message, with an injection of humor:

> *Lynn,*
>
> *Your projected budget was excellent. It was well written, well organized, and comprehensive. You anticipated several expense categories I might have overlooked. Maybe my wife and I can use your services for our household budget—which we never seem to get right!*
> *Thanks for always coming through for us.*
>
> *Bob*

Writing to a Mixed Readership

When writing to a mixed group of supervisors, peers, and subordinates (as with a divisionwide report), treat all readers respectfully as key people in the organization. Never risk offending a person in any of those groups.

To play it safe, follow the tone you normally use for your supervisors. Exude confidence in your abilities, come across as a team player, and convey that you appreciate what's important to each group of readers. This could mean increasing revenues (for top executives), providing ample support staff (for mid-level managers), and ensuring satisfactory working conditions (for administrative personnel).

Embellish Good News

The right words can generate excitement and motivate employees at all levels, especially when there's good news to share. Don't waste any opportunity to help others feel better about the company and their role in it.

Here are two very different examples of the same message:

◆ *We're meeting on October 20 to discuss the positive results just reported from the second quarter. Among the results are revenues that set a record as the highest ever achieved. At the meeting we will give recognition to all who made contributions. We'll also talk about improving on these results this quarter.*

That's dull and entirely lifeless. There's no enthusiasm or sense of accomplishment. The record-setting revenues—a great feat—come across merely as a discussion item for the upcoming meeting agenda.

◆ *Great news! We achieved record-high revenues for the second quarter, and we're meeting on October 20 to recognize all of your hard work and to see how we can do even better this quarter.*

That's much livelier, much more exciting and congratulatory. We all wish there were more positive news to report, so when there is cause for celebration, use the opportunity to help others feel good and to improve morale.

Show Enthusiasm for Others' Ideas

When reacting to someone else's ideas, it's possible to show enthusiasm, indifference, and everything in between. If you quickly dismiss others' suggestions without carefully considering them, you'll be viewed

POINTER

Write with enthusiasm for others' ideas to show you're a team player.

as a me-first employee who doesn't want anyone else to be recognized for good ideas. An enthusiastic tone can demonstrate that you're a team player with more interest in the good of the company than in your own success, and that can go a long way in enhancing relationships with people at all levels of the organization. Let's look at an example:

◆ **Indifferent, judgmental response:**

> *Jennifer,*
>
> *I received your email about scheduling breakfasts each Thursday to brainstorm marketing concepts with the engineering team. This probably won't work, given our schedules. We need an entirely different approach.*
>
> *Steve*

◆ **Enthusiastic, supportive response:**

> *Jennifer,*
>
> *Weekly breakfasts with the engineering team to brainstorm marketing ideas could work very well. We may need to iron out some scheduling issues, but this approach has great potential. Call me so we can discuss the specifics.*
>
> *Steve*

Disagree Without Talking Down to Your Reader

If you're asked for feedback on an idea that you believe is flawed—an idea from someone at any level—use tact to explain why the idea won't work. Avoid being judgmental or condescending. See the different tone in these two versions of the same message:

◆ **Condescending, judgmental:**

> *Dan,*
>
> *Your proposal to redistrict the Western sales territories to lower operating expenses doesn't make much sense when*

you examine the facts. First of all,
there's no way the Northwest sales reps
will relocate 175 miles from Seattle to
Portland. Many are settled with fami-
lies, a fact that you should be aware of.
And you never thought about the added
travel expenses. Do you know how much
harder it is to get flights from Portland?
The additional costs would dwarf the
small savings in office rent.

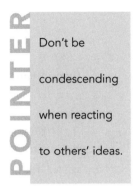

Don't be condescending when reacting to others' ideas.

Furthermore, your recommendation to promote Mike
Larson to sales manager will never see the light of day.
Although Mike has some innovative ideas, he has only
two years' experience in our industry! There's no way we
can give him such responsibility.

Let's meet later this week and see if we can come up
with something better.

Ron

◆ **Tactful in explaining shortcomings:**

Dan,

Thanks for your proposal on redistricting the Western
sales territories. I agree that we need to lower operating
expenses. There are a few issues we need to look at con-
cerning your plan.

First, Mike Larson, who—as you stated—has devel-
oped many innovative ideas, has only two years' experi-
ence in our industry, and senior management may not
let him take the reins in Portland.

Second, the Northwest sales reps, many of whom are
settled with families, might resist relocating from Seattle
to Portland, 175 miles away.

Travel expenses may be considerably higher, given the
difficulty in getting nonstop flights in and out of Port-
land. These additional costs may outweigh the savings
in rent.

STEP 7

Let's meet later this week. We should be able to put our heads together and come up with other ideas.

Thanks,

Ron

The second version addresses exactly the same shortcomings inherent in Dan's ideas, but it does so in a more collegial tone. The writer acknowledges Dan's correct ideas (that costs need to be reduced and that Mike has offered some innovative ideas) before pointing out the faults in his judgments. The overall tone is cooperative and gently corrective, with a statement of conviction that Dan will be able to contribute other workable ideas in a meeting with Ron.

Empathize When Delivering Bad News

At one time or another, many of you have been customers who've contacted companies to request refunds, rebates, discounts, and other perks you believe are owed to you. If you discover that you're not getting whatever you think you deserve, for whatever reason, you're unhappy. If you're the one delivering that bad news, you should realize that it's unlikely you'll ever make the customer entirely happy. But you can temper your bad-news message to show that you understand the person's troubles.

Here are a few tips for delivering negative news:
- ◆ Don't hide bad news.
- ◆ Don't patronize the reader (for example, don't write *We love our loyal customers* or *We treat all employees like family*).
- ◆ Put yourself in the reader's shoes and imagine how you'd feel in that situation.

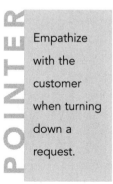

POINTER

Empathize with the customer when turning down a request.

Below are examples of ineffective and effective ways to tell small business owner

Lauren Thompson that her LCD projector is no longer under warranty and will cost $500 to repair. The projector malfunctioned just hours before an out-of-town new business presentation, forcing her to rent a projector at the last moment. Lauren has sent an email, expressing her dissatisfaction that the product had failed just 15 months after she purchased it and has requested that the manufacturer cover the cost of the repair or send her a new projector.

◆ **Impersonal and ineffective:**

> *With regret, I must tell you that your LCD projector is no longer under warranty and we cannot repair the switch malfunction you reported. The projector is guaranteed for 12 months, and your problem occurred 15 months after the purchase date.*
>
> *We did offer an extended warranty for $49.99 that would have covered the machine for an additional 24 months, but you declined that offer.*
>
> *Our company apologizes for any inconvenience or unanticipated expense as a result of the machine's malfunction. We have many new LCD projector models available (see the link to our website), and I'd be happy to have one of our sales reps contact you to discuss which is best for your needs and to discuss the extended warranty.*
>
> *Sincerely,*
>
> *Bill Sullivan*
>
> *Customer Service Manager*

◆ **Empathetic:**

> *Dear Ms. Thompson,*
>
> *What an inopportune time for your LCD projector to break down. I hope your presentation with the rented machine was successful—and that you turned the prospect into a client.*
>
> *We do our best to build high-quality machines, but sometimes make mistakes in the process. Unfortunately, we can't bend the rules on warranties. I wish we could.*

What I'd like to do is research other models in our inventory and offer you the best discounts available—those usually reserved for our large corporate customers who purchase 25 or more machines a year. I'll also offer the extended warranty for $25, a 50 percent savings. Give me a week and I'll call you to let you know what's available and give you details on the discounts.

Please call me if you have questions.

Sincerely,

Bill Sullivan

It's unlikely that Bill's first letter will appease Lauren, and there's very little chance that she'll purchase any more products from Bill's company. The second one empathizes with Lauren's circumstances as a businesswoman, expresses interest in her success, and commits the writer to an active role in solving the problem in a way that may satisfy all parties. Plus it sets a much warmer tone. That email could win Lauren over, or at least show her that Bill and others at the company care about the people who use their products. Notice that Bill does *not* get to the point right away. Instead, he begins by putting himself in the customer's shoes.

Select the Right Words

Write text that speaks to people one-on-one rather than as a crowd. This means using words such as *you, me, we,* and *us,* which help instill a sense of teamwork and camaraderie when writing a message for internal distribution and which express personal empathy when writing to customers and other external readers.

In many situations, you'll want to choose words or phrases that soften the impact of your message. When the point you must make can sting the reader, always remember to choose more gentle words to convey the same information. Look at tool 7.1 for some examples.

TOOL 7.1

Words and Phrases That Soften the Impact

Stings	Softer Approach
Unacceptable	Unsuitable
Not important, unimportant	Minor
Your presentation was dull.	Your presentation could have been a bit more engaging.
Your proposal missed some vital points.	Your proposal should have included some key points.
You never returned my call.	I haven't been able to reach you.
I don't like your idea.	I have some concerns about your idea.
Your email confused me.	I wasn't sure how to interpret your email.
Your plan failed.	We had some difficulty implementing your plan.
You left 25 employees off the registration list.	For some reason, 25 employees were left off the registration list.
You screwed up the report, just like last month.	The errors you made on this report are the same ones you made on last month's report.

Your Turn

Crafting the right tone is difficult in situations where readers will not be happy with your central message. For example, it takes practice to empathize with angry customers or to criticize without being condescending. These exercises will help hone your skills in writing with an appropriate tone.

1. Rewrite the following email sent from a supervisor to her subordinates. Make your tone more productive than this writer's antagonistic, condescending tone.

Haven't you people been paying attention lately? This is the third week in a row that parts have been prepared for shipping without purchase orders. I keep telling you: If there's no purchase order, the shipment gets delayed—and that makes customers unhappy! We can't have this! I need all of you to meet in the conference room Thursday at 8 a.m. sharp so that, once again, I can explain the procedures. This meeting is **mandatory,** *so I'll expect you there, on time!*

2. This email, suggesting a $25,000 investment in new color printers, was written from one department head to three other department heads. Rewrite it to convince the CFO to spend the money.

    You all agree that the printers are not producing sharp colors, which is hurting our proposals. I've done some research, and, for $25,000, we can get five of the latest-model printers that can produce 35 color pages per minute. Think of how impressive our proposals can be with beautiful color charts, graphs, and photos! Plus, it could help our closing ratio. I'd say that out of every 10 prospects, we could close two more sales. Let me know what you think.

3. Revise this email, written in response to a suggestion to double spending on trade magazine advertising, so it's less condescending but still explains the flaws in the proposal.

    Lou, there's no way spending twice as much on trade magazine ads will produce the desired return-on-investment. As you should be aware, readership for print magazines is way down the past few years. Our customers, like those in many industries, have shifted to the web. Print is dying a slow death, Lou! It's an online world, so if we're going to get any bang for the dollar, it should be with email blasts, search-word marketing, banner ads, and other online tactics. I

suggest you think this over and come back to us with
a new plan that incorporates online marketing.

4. You just received a letter from a customer who's angry that his snowblower didn't work when he tried clearing a 2-foot snowfall from his driveway. As a result of the machine's failure, the customer was forced to spend $200 on a plowing service. He wants the company to pay for the $800 snowblower repair, although the warranty expired three months ago. The customer also wants your company to reimburse him for the plowing expense. Write a letter explaining that the company can't pay for either expense, but do it in a way that conveys your empathy with his situation.

The Next Step

In addition to carefully choosing and using a tone that expresses empathy and produces the results you want, you need to exhibit your professionalism in the way you compose your text. That requires, among other skills, a reasonable command of grammar. We'll address that topic in Step 8: Put Your Best Grammar on the Page.

STEP 7

NOTES

STEP

7

Put Your Best Grammar on the Page

OVERVIEW

Review of basic punctuation

Guidance on the essential rules of grammar

Tips for avoiding common mistakes in word usage

Leaving out a comma or using a colon when you should've used a semicolon won't ruin your career. But a document laden with mis-used words, verbs that don't agree with their subjects, inconsistent tenses, incorrect punctuation, and other mistakes can make you look unprofessional or lazy.

Grammar is one of those areas that readers notice more if it's wrong than if it's right. You probably won't earn a big bonus for us-ing correct grammar and syntax (word arrangement), but you will create text that's clear and that helps achieve the desired results.

If you know your grammar skills are top-notch, skim this step or skip it entirely. But if you struggle with grammar or need a refresher, study the key rules and the examples that follow. They won't address more advanced aspects of grammar (like gerunds, participles, and nonstandard verb phrases), but they will explain how to determine what's right and wrong in your business communication.

In many cases, you don't need to memorize grammar rules; just use the same common sense that prevents you from comparing

STEP 8

apples with oranges. For rules not addressed in this step, consult a grammar book or website. I frequently use dictionaries, grammar guides, and on-line resources to look up spelling and proper usage. See the Resources section at the back of this book for some suggested reference works.

A Review of Basic Punctuation

For those who like to start at the beginning, tool 8.1 offers a review of basic punctuation. Those of you who are confident of your skill in punctuation can skip ahead to the next section.

TOOL 8.1

The Rules of Basic Punctuation

Comma

* Separates independent clauses (complete sentences) joined by a conjunction: *I enjoy Italian food, but I don't like seafood.*

* Separates introductory phrase or clause from the rest of the sentence: *Knowing her deadline was tight, she worked the entire weekend.*

* Sets apart items in a series: *The report included ideas on marketing, operations, and customer service.* (Notice that there should be a comma before the conjunction "and" because the final two items are separate.)

* Sets off a phrase that describes a subject but is not necessary to complete the sentence: *Steve Jones, who was hired six months ago, has done an excellent job.*

* Is always placed inside quotation marks: *"I'll complete the report by tomorrow afternoon," she told her boss.*

Colon

* Indicates a stop followed by an explanation: *He figured out how to impress his boss: develop an Internet marketing plan.*

* Indicates a stop followed by a list: *She placed three items on her desk: a stapler, a magnifying glass, and a stuffed yellow lizard.*

* Never directly follows a verb.

continued on next page

STEP 8

Tool 8.1, continued

Semicolon

* Joins two sentences that have similar construction: *Last year's annual report was 50 pages long; this year's report was only 35 pages.*

* Joins items in a comma-separated series to avoid confusion: *The sales team's hectic month included trips to Wilmington, Delaware; Athens, Ohio; Portland, Maine; and Fairfield, New Jersey.*

Hyphen

* Joins two or more words that serve as an adjective modifying a noun: *The manager suggested that the conference be divided into three-hour sessions.* Without the hyphen in *three-hour,* the reader might assume the manager suggested three 60-minute sessions.

Dash

* May be used in place of commas to set off a long phrase: *The first-line manager's proposal—which explained how to use the new sales generation program that's designed to double the number of leads in six months— was embraced by all the senior executives.*

* Sets information apart with emphasis: *By speaking up to the boss, the customer service rep received a 15 percent raise—a totally unexpected outcome, given the supervisor's track record on salaries.*

Parentheses

* Sets off information that is relevant but need not be emphasized: *She was exhausted after a long road trip to many Ohio cities (including Akron, Columbus, Dayton, and Toledo) to visit her key clients.*

Sometimes It's OK to Break a Big Old Rule

Because it's more fun (I know, grammar isn't really fun) to learn what you *can* do than to learn what you can't, let's start by shattering an old rule from grammar school, high school, and college. It's OK to start a sentence with a conjunction like *and, but,* or *because.* Conjunctions can provide context for what you're about to write and can help you make a less abrupt transition from one sentence to another or from one paragraph to another. Using conjunctions to begin your sentence may add to the gentle rhythm of your words (Step 5). Here are some examples:

◆ ***Because* to give context:** *Because we've received so many customer complaints, I suggest a meeting next week to review procedures for handling calls.*

◆ ***And* to unify sentences:** *Over the past 18 months, our company has been able to increase revenues and control costs while three of our largest competitors have seen their revenues drop significantly. And we're poised to continue this success over the next five years.*

Note that the two sentences in that example are too long to combine into one sentence joined by *and*. Beginning the second sentence with the conjunction carries the thought forward.

◆ ***But* to unify paragraphs:** *For the past five years, direct mail had proven to be highly successful. In that time, we were able to increase market share and generate 10 to 15 percent more leads than in the prior year. Everyone, including the vice president of marketing, expected this trend to continue for at least five more years.*

But over the past two years, the number of new leads from direct mail has fallen off dramatically. The marketing director contends that many purchasing managers ignore snail mail and look instead for online offers.

Starting that second paragraph with *but over the past two years* provides a logical transition from the previous paragraph's discussion of the successful direct mail program.

Follow the Essential Rules of Grammar and Syntax

As energizing as it can be to break a rule, most time-tested grammar rules do need to be followed. Here are some of the most important ones.

Make Nouns and Pronouns Agree in Number

If the subject of a sentence is singular, any pronoun that replaces that subject also must be singular; if the subject is plural, a replacing pronoun must be plural.

- **Singular:** *Rita Young, the newest branch **manager**, was happy with **her** commission check.*
- **Plural:** *All four branch **managers** were happy with **their** commission checks.*

Make Verbs and Subjects Agree in Number

Singular subjects require singular verbs; plural subjects require plural verbs.

- **Wrong: *There's** too many conference calls.*
- **Right: *There are** too many conference calls.*

When choosing a singular or plural verb to agree in number with the subject of a sentence, ignore any phrases that follow the subject. The word immediately before the verb determines the number of the verb *only* if it's really the subject. Don't be fooled by how it sounds—double-check yourself to see that you know which word is the subject of the sentence. In the following examples, the subjects and verbs are in boldface type.

- **Wrong:** *The **team** of sales reps **are** committed to success.*
- **Right:** *The **team** of sales reps **is** committed to success.*
- **Wrong: *Each** of the branch managers **agree** that customer service must improve.*
- **Right: *Each** of the branch managers **agrees** that customer service must improve.*
- **Wrong:** *The new security **procedures,** which offer much-needed protection, **has been** difficult for most employees to learn.*
- **Right:** *The new security **procedures,** which offer much-needed protection, **have been** difficult for most employees to learn.*

Keep Tenses Consistent

Past, present, and future tenses are easily muddled in business writing. The goal is not to shift tenses in the flow of the sentence. Here are some sample pairs of sentences, one wrong and one right.

- **Shifted tense:** *As soon as he completed the report, he **walked** out of the room and **was heading** to the local pub to join his co-workers.* The shift here is from past (*walked*) to present tense (*was heading*).

- **Consistent tense:** *As soon as he completed the report, he **walked** out of the room and **headed** to the local pub to join his co-workers.*

- **Shifted tense:** *If Lou **would pay** more attention to his employees' needs, he **can be** an excellent manager.*

- **Consistent tense:** *If Lou **pays** more attention to his employees' needs, he **can be** an excellent manager.*

- **Shifted tense:** *In 2006, the CEO **said** she **is** fed up with the bookkeeping mistakes.*

- **Consistent tense:** *In 2006, the CEO **said** she **was** fed up with the bookkeeping mistakes.*

Don't Put Words or Phrases in the Wrong Positions

Your message can confuse readers if words are out of place. Here are some confusing examples and instructions for fixing them.

- **Confusing:** *The sales manager closed the deal with a real estate firm using an innovative approach to web marketing.*

In that example, the reader could make one of two assumptions: that the sales manager presented an innovative approach to the real estate firm or that the real estate firm was already using the innovative approach to web marketing.

- **Clear:** *Using an innovative approach to web marketing, the sales manager closed the deal with a real estate firm.*

In that revised version, moving the phrase *using an innovative approach to web marketing* to the beginning of the sentence ties it directly to the sales manager.

STEP
8

In the following example, the phrase *last month* is poorly positioned.

◆ **Confusing:** *The southeast sales team that was reviewing the most recent leads last month suggested that account reps target only prospects within a 45-mile radius of the office.*

Did the team make the suggestion last month, or did they review the leads last month? This clarifies it:

◆ **Clear:** *After reviewing the most recent leads from last month, the southeast sales team suggested that account reps target only prospects within a 45-mile radius of the office.*

Use *and* to Clarify Connections

Leaving the word *and* out of a sentence where it would identify relationships among items is a common mistake. Here's an example:

◆ **Incorrect:** *We chose Phoenix for its delightful climate, its large number of skilled workers, the city's willingness to build roads, malls and communication systems.*

There are two problems with that sentence. First, the internal punctuation is wrong (semicolons should separate the reasons Phoenix was chosen because one of the reasons is a phrase that contains commas). Second, the word *and* is needed to show that there are three reasons for the choice of Phoenix.

The "missing-and" problem happens most often when you're enumerating a set of structurally parallel items (in the example above, the reasons for choosing Phoenix). To avoid the problem, begin by listing the items:

1. delightful climate
2. large number of skilled workers
3. city's willingness to build
   a. roads
   a. malls
   a. communication systems.

With that list, you see there are three reasons (climate, workers, and willingness to build). The third reason has three items within it (roads, malls, communication systems). When you know what your sentence includes, it's simple to write it clearly and accurately:

◆ **Correct:** *We chose Phoenix for (1) its desirable location; (2) its large number of skilled workers; and (3) the city's willingness to build roads, malls, and communication systems.*

Don't Dangle Your Participle

I don't like to use grammar-speak, but I've got to do it this one time. A participle is a word that has the features of both a verb and an adjective, and a phrase that includes a participial usually modifies a noun. A participial phrase is said to "dangle" when it's not physically located immediately before the noun it describes. When you look at the following examples, you'll recognize the problem and you'll realize how often this happens in speaking and writing.

◆ **Wrong:** *Being an avid NASCAR fan, a ticket to the qualifying heat delighted Paul.*

◆ **Wrong:** *While driving to a business meeting, Sue's car overheated and she arrived 45 minutes late.*

See the problems? A ticket is not a NASCAR fan (Paul is), and Sue's car wasn't driving to the meeting (Sue was). The problem is that the descriptive phrase immediately precedes the wrong word. Let's correct those danglers:

◆ **Right:** *Being an avid NASCAR fan, Paul was delighted with a ticket to the qualifying heat.*

◆ **Right:** *While driving to a business meeting, Sue found that her car was overheating and she arrived 45 minutes late.*

You may find it easier to rewrite the sentence without the introductory modifying phrase. Here's an example.

◆ **Right:** *Sue's car overheated on the way to the new business meeting, so she arrived 45 minutes late.*

Use Parallel Structure

Parallelism—writing similar groups of thoughts in the same pattern—is not only good grammar; it also makes much it easier for the reader to digest the message. A parallel structure gives text a rhythm and a logical flow. (See Step 5 for more about rhythm and flow.) One of the simplest places to demonstrate parallelism (or the lack of it) is with bulleted items, so let's start there. Consider this list and see if you can identify what's not parallel:

To improve communication, I suggest
- *meetings conducted once a week*
- *hold conference calls each month*
- *I'd recommend budget reports to be produced every quarter.*

The first item in the list begins with a noun (*meetings*), the second item begins with a verb (*hold*), and the third item is a full sentence. And neither the second nor third item flows grammatically from the introductory phrase *I suggest*. The bulleted items don't have a parallel structure. There are two steps to correcting that example. First, identify the type of word that must follow the introductory phrase. In this case, it can be a noun or a verb with an "-ing" ending. Second, write the bullet points so each begins with a noun (meetings, conference calls, budget reports) or with an -ing verb (conducting, holding, producing). Here's the parallel version using nouns:

To improve communication, I suggest
- *weekly meetings*
- *monthly conference calls*
- *quarterly budget reports.*

And here's the parallel version using -ing verbs:

To improve communication, I suggest
- *conducting weekly meetings*
- *holding monthly conference calls*
- *producing quarterly budget reports.*

In other cases, parallel bulleted items all could be commands, like this:

In the next two weeks, all division heads must
- *schedule performance reviews for the next six months*

◆ submit travel plans for the next three months

◆ write the first draft of next quarter's budget.

Using a parallel structure pertains to paragraph text, too. Although writing concise text requires eliminating unnecessary words, sometimes an extra word is needed to ensure clarity. In many cases, that means repeating conjunctions, verbs, and prepositions to help the reader grasp the points more easily. Let's look at a sample sentence:

At the annual meeting, the head of security was recognized for his outstanding service to the firm by the chief operating officer, who had known him for 15 years, and the vice president of human resources, who had hired him 20 years ago.

Simply repeating the word *by* makes the sentence parallel and more easily understood:

*At the annual meeting, the head of security was recognized for his outstanding service to the firm **by** the chief operating officer, who had known him for 15 years, and **by** the vice president of human resources, who had hired him 20 years ago.*

Here's another example where one little word repeated two times will make all the difference. Can you see what that word is?

At the start of the meeting, the IT director discussed the new software program, training schedule, and most critical compliance issues.

The answer is *the*:

*At the start of the meeting, the chief information officer discussed **the** new software program, **the** training schedule, and **the** most critical compliance issues.*

The meaning doesn't change when *the* is repeated before each of the topics discussed, but the sentence becomes more coherent and easier to understand.

And, finally, a nonparallel example that can be corrected in either of two ways:

The executive assistant's main responsibilities are to schedule meetings for the president, plan all events for the board of directors, and to order supplies for the executive team.

First, the word *to* can be added before *plan* to form three parallel phrases:

*The executive assistant's main responsibilities are **to** schedule meetings for the president, **to** plan all events for the board of directors, and **to** order supplies for the executive team.*

Second, the verbs can be changed to noun forms and the three uses of *to* can be eliminated:

*The executive assistant's main responsibilities are **scheduling** meetings for the president, **planning** all events for the board of directors, and **ordering** supplies for the executive team.*

Write Complete Sentences

One of the worst mistakes in business writing is the failure to construct complete sentences. It's a sign that the writer either is sloppy or never has bothered to learn basic grammar rules.

The usual problem is that several related thoughts are strung together without the appropriate punctuation or transition words, or that several unrelated thoughts are combined. They form nothing cohesive. With minor revisions, the thoughts could be joined smoothly and logically, or each thought could stand as a complete sentence. Here's an example.

◆ **Wrong:** *Larry, the branch manager, was born in Baltimore in 1960, it was much different then before the Inner Harbor was developed.*

- **Right, rewritten as two sentences:** *Larry, the branch manager, was born in Baltimore in 1960. That city was much different then, before the Inner Harbor was developed.*
- **Right, rewritten as one sentence:** *Larry, the branch manager, was born in Baltimore in 1960, a time before the Inner Harbor was developed and when the city was much different.*

Another common mistake in trying to construct a cohesive sentence is using *however* as a conjunction. Here's an example:

- **Wrong:** *The board members said that Karen's marketing plan was well written with innovative ideas, however, they agreed that several important details were omitted.*
- **Right, as two sentences:** *The board members said that Karen's marketing plan was well written with innovative ideas. However, they agreed that several important details were omitted.*
- **Right, as one sentence:** *The board members said that Karen's marketing plan was well written with innovative ideas, but they agreed that several important details were omitted.*

One last (surprising?) point: sometimes, sentence fragments are OK. In some cases—as a reaction to another sentence—it's okay to use a sentence fragment for dramatic effect. Here are a couple of examples:

- *The accounting team has pledged to be more careful when reporting figures.* **Every last digit.**
- *What will it take for the northeast division to meet its sales goals?* **A lot more effort.**

The only caveat about sentence fragments: use them sparingly.

Use *e.g.* and *i.e.* Correctly

This rule is broken in so many documents. If you mean "for example," use *e.g.* Use *i.e.* only if you mean "in other words" or "that is." These abbreviations have come to English from Latin: *e.g.* is the shortened form of *exempli gratia* and *i.e.* is the shortened form of *id est*. Most formal writing doesn't use abbreviated word forms, but more casual business communications do use them, especially in parenthetical clauses. Be sure to insert a comma after the second period in each of these abbreviations. Here are two examples of correct usage:

◆ *Steve prefers brochures with bright colors (e.g., orange, pink, and green).*

◆ *Columns for the company newsletter should be short (i.e., 300 words or less).*

Watch Where You Put That Apostrophe

An apostrophe is a mark inserted in a word or between two words to take the place of letters that have been dropped: *do not* becomes *don't, she will* becomes *she'll.* The mark is also used to show the possessive case: *Aziz's assignment, the boys' lockers.* So simple . . . until it comes to *it is* or the possessive of *it.* This may be the most-often-made error in written text. Here is the rule as plainly as I can state it: If you mean to shorten "it is," use an apostrophe to combine the two words and take the place of the dropped letter *i—it's cold out here* or *it's never going to rain.* If, instead, you're explaining that some *it* possesses some thing, write *its* with no apostrophe. Here's an example: *Luisa is late because her team hasn't finished its meeting.*

Write in the Active Voice

In Step 4, I explained the benefit of using active verbs to engage your reader. When you use active verbs, you're writing in the active voice. Similarly, when using passive verbs, you're using the passive voice. Passive verb phrases require more words than do active ones, and they introduce a degree of separation between the doer and the action. Hesitation is the very subtle message conveyed by the passive voice. Here are a few examples of passive voice corrected to active voice:

◆ **Passive:** *My business trip to Rio de Janeiro is one I'll always remember.*

- **Active:** *I'll always remember my business trip to Rio de Janeiro*
- **Passive:** *It was her suggestion that all employees on the late shift take a 20-minute break every four hours.*
- **Active:** *She suggested that all employees on the late shift take a 20-minute break every four hours.*

Connect the Verb with the Correct Noun

Sometimes verbs that seem to be appropriate are incorrect. For example, if you write *The staff was distressed to hear that vacation days would be cut in half,* someone is sure to point out that a vacation day—like every day—is 24 hours and isn't going to become 12 hours. It's the *number of vacation days* that would be cut in half.

Avoid Common Word Usage Errors

Beyond the cut-and-dry rules of grammar, there's the issue of word choice. Perfect grammar surrounding the wrong word won't fix your mistake. In lots of cases, the errors occur because very different words are spelled very similarly. In other cases, it's simply a matter of not knowing the correct meaning of words you're trying to use. (See tool 8.2 for a list of commonly misused words and examples of correct usage.)

For example, let's look at the words *affect* and *effect*. These words are confused and misused frequently. But when you understand that *affect* is a verb and *effect* is a noun, your confusion diminishes.

- **Right:** *Poor morale negatively affects productivity.*
- **Right:** *Poor morale can have a devastating effect on productivity.*

There are, however, two occasions when those words change places. *Affect* becomes a noun when the writer is describing a person's visible emotion:

The psychologist noticed his affect during the cognitive tests.

STEP **8**

TOOL 8.2

Commonly Misused Words and Phrases and Examples of Correct Usage

Accept/Except	◆ He *accepts* your proposal. ◆ Each report was correct *except* the monthly sales report.
Advice/Advise	◆ Her *advice* is critical. ◆ We *advise* employees to report expenses accurately.
Aggravate/Irritate	◆ The employee's frequent lateness *aggravated* the tension among his co-workers. ◆ The receptionist's behavior *irritated* the visitors in the lobby.
All ready/Already	◆ The budget was *all ready* for the president's review. ◆ By the end of the third quarter, the operations budget *already* was spent.
Among/Between	◆ He worked *among* many conscientious employees. ◆ She planned to eat lunch *between* the two meetings.
Amount/Number	◆ The *amount* of information she gathered was sufficient for her report. ◆ Judging by the *number* of people in line, we expected they'd run out of tickets.
Any one/Anyone	◆ *Any one* of you could become the next manager. ◆ *Anyone* who works hard will succeed.
Bad/Badly	◆ We always have *bad* weather this time of year. ◆ The HR department softball team played *badly*.

STEP 8

continued on next page

115

Tool 8.2, continued

Bring/Take	◆ The supervisor asked Ted to **bring** her a newspaper each morning.
	◆ Ted offered to **take** the bundle of papers to the recycling center.
Composed/Comprised	◆ Three realtors, two developers, and one land manager **composed** the zoning board.
	◆ The company's Detroit complex **comprises** three office buildings, a laboratory, and a distribution center.
Device/Devise	◆ We need a **device** to hold up the screen.
	◆ She **devised** a plan to sell more insurance.
Discreet/Discrete	◆ The team manager made a **discreet** exit during the meeting.
	◆ Payroll and Benefits are two **discrete** departments.
Ensure/Insure	◆ Purchasing a home security system will **ensure** a better night's sleep.
	◆ You should **insure** your California home against earthquakes and mudslides.
Explicit/Implicit	◆ The job description was very **explicit** in describing weight and height requirements.
	◆ **Implicit** in the ad was the notion that jogging was a pleasant experience.
Fewer/Less	◆ She took five **fewer** business trips this year.
	◆ With her promotion to senior vice president, she had **less** time for socializing.
Good/Well	◆ His concentration was not **good**.
	◆ The controller doesn't feel **well** this morning.
Into/In to	◆ The boss walked **into** the room.
	◆ Turn your reports **in to** me.

It's/Its	• *It's* time to write the budget analysis. • The company and *its* policies are well known.
Lose/Loose	• If you *lose* your pen, you won't be able to sign your check. • The new shoes were very *loose* on her feet.
May Be/Maybe	• We *may be* late. • *Maybe* we'll be early today.
Precede/Proceed	• The letter A *precedes* the letter B. • You may *proceed* to the conference room.
Respectfully/ Respectively	• She *respectfully* responded to the request. • The CD and DVD cost $14.99 and $17.99, *respectively*.
Slow/Slowly	• This clock always runs *slow*. • The cat *slowly* stalked the robin across the yard.
Than/Then	• Today's presentation was two hours longer *than* last week's program. • He stood up, walked around the conference table three times, and *then* left.
That/Which	• The *Wall Street Journal that* I left at your door this morning is the most recent edition. • The *Wall Street Journal, which* covers a broad spectrum of issues, is well written.
Their/There/They're	• *Their* grammar is very good. • The supervisor should sit *there*. • *They're* very proud of this year's results.
Your/You're	• *Your* assignment is to write a paragraph about your work. • *You're* the last person to submit the report.

STEP
8

Effect becomes a verb when the writer is using it to mean "bring about":

> *With his policies, the new CEO hoped to effect great change in the organization.*

Those less-common uses of *affect* and *effect* seldom occur in business documents, but it's good to be prepared.

Your Turn

Using correct grammar takes practice and the willingness to look up the right usage in a resource book or on a website. Though nobody expects you to be perfect, you should avoid mistakes that could make you appear uneducated or lazy. The exercises below will give you some quick practice on aspects of grammar where mistakes are commonly made.

1. Circle the word with the apostrophe in the correct position:
   a. *The daycare manager misplaced the* **children's/childrens'** *favorite toys.*
   b. *Maria lost all the data on her laptop computer when* **it's/its** *hard drive crashed.*
   c. *The* **supervisor's/supervisors'** *best asset is his technical knowledge.*
   d. *The head of operations,* **whose/who's** *subordinates work hard, earned another production award.*
   e. **It's/Its** *hard to keep morale strong during a corporate upheaval.*
   f. *Please review both proposals—***Mike's and Jennifer's/Mike and Jennifer's***—by Tuesday.*

2. Circle the correct word for noun–pronoun agreement or verb–subject agreement:
   a. *The team of supervisors always* **exceed/exceeds** *expectations.*
   b. *Each of the section managers* **agree/agrees** *that service has improved.*

c. *We believe in the XYZ Company and **its/their** people.*

d. *The new evacuation procedures, which could offer much-needed peace of mind, **has/have** met with strong opposition.*

e. *Susan, along with six of her co-workers, **exercise/exercises** every evening after work.*

f. *Susan and six of her co-workers **exercise/exercises** every evening after work.*

3. Circle the correct word—*that* or *which:*

a. *The first draft of our annual report, **that/which** had many mistakes, had to be rewritten.*

b. *In Search of Excellence was one of those business books **that/which** millions read in the early 1990s.*

c. *Dallas is the only southwest city **that/which** the salespeople will travel to this year.*

d. *The new security software, **that/which** continues to confuse the account coordinators, needs to be updated.*

4. Correct the mistakes in each of these sentences:

a. *There was a heated debate between the three team leaders.*

b. *With the large amount of new hires in the third quarter, another employee orientation was scheduled.*

c. *He traveled 3,000 miles to visit ABC Consulting's Juan Santos, which had been his client for 16 years.*

d. *We had 50 less errors in the third quarter than we had in the second quarter.*

e. *At the annual meeting, the CEO announced that, effective immediately, vacation days would increase by 15 percent.*

5. Rewrite so the bulleted copy is in a parallel format:

We came up with some excellent ideas at this morning's meeting. Below is a review of some of the important next steps:

◆ *Getting managers to be more decisive by pairing them with mentors, each with five or more years of experience*

STEP **8**

- *Managers should get educated on new products through a 45-minute presentation at the start of each weekly meeting*
- *Encourage managers to seek each other's help more often.*

6. Rewrite this sentence to create a parallel structure:

The chief marketing officer's most important assets are her ability to produce effective magazine ads, generate consistent leads, and to open up new territories.

For the answers to questions 1 through 4, look below.

The Next Step

Writing clear, concise, and compelling documents—with proper grammar—enables you to deliver powerful messages that help achieve your goals. But writing perfect text the first time is rare. To ensure that your message comes out the way you want it to, you'll probably need to edit your text. That's discussed in Step 9: Edit, Rewrite, and Refine.

1. (a) children's, (b) its, (c) supervisor's, (d) whose, (e) It's, (f) Mike's and Jennifer's.

2. (a) exceeds, (b) agrees, (c) its, (d) have, (e) exercises, (f) exercise.

3. (a) which, (b) that, (c) that, (d) which.

4. (a) Change *between* to *among* because more than two parties are involved. (b) Change *amount* to *number* because the new hires are quantifiable. (c) Assuming Juan had been the client, *which* should be changed to *who*. (d) *Less*, which is used only with amounts that can't be quantified precisely, should be changed to *fewer* because a specific number of errors is cited. (e) Add *the number of before vacation* to clarify what would increase.

STEP
8

NOTES

_____

_____

_____

_____

_____

_____

_____

_____

_____

_____

_____

_____

_____

_____

_____

_____

_____

_____

_____

_____

_____

STEP
8

Edit, Rewrite, and Refine

OVERVIEW

Discussion of the three-stage editing process

Instructions for revising the message, improving the organization, and polishing the mechanics

Examples of rough-draft, redlined, and final documents

The first thing to remember about editing is *not* to do it while you're writing the first draft. It's better to complete the first draft by letting the words pour out so you don't interrupt your natural flow of ideas. (See Step 2: Know Where You're Taking Your Readers for a discussion of free-writing.) When you've completed the first draft, that's the time to begin refining your document.

In this step, we'll look at the editing *process* rather than at specific editorial changes you may want to make to your document. Those specifics have been covered in the earlier steps of this book.

Take a Break Before You Revise Your Draft

It's easy to get attached to the words you write and the way you've written them. That's a great reason to put some space between the first draft and the editing process. Even a couple of hours can cool your (probably unwarranted) passion for your draft and can increase your willingness to see and fix its shortcomings. Whenever possible, write the first draft and put it aside. Refocus your concentration on something else and come back to the document several hours later or even the next day.

When ridiculously tight deadlines—like in the next 30 minutes—force you to write quickly and leave you little time to review, take at least a few minutes to read the document to yourself to catch obvious mistakes in spelling, grammar, and word usage and to ensure it makes sense.

Read from the Recipient's Point of View

To become an effective editor, you *must* be critical of your own text and make the necessary changes. When you're ready to revise your document, here's the first truth: to write better, you need to know what will *read* better. (Apologies for the ungrammatical use of the word *read*—sometimes you have to break a rule to make a point.)

If you want to write better, know what will *read* better to others.

To evaluate how readable and understandable your document will be, put yourself behind your readers' glasses. Will they find the document clear, concise, and organized? Will they figure out the situation that prompted your writing it—the context? Will they make sense of your data? Will they take the action or support the position you're recommending?

The best way to answer those questions for yourself as you begin the editing is to read the words out loud. If something sounds confusing, it probably is. If you don't think the words flow well, the reader won't think they flow well either.

Follow the Three-Stage Editing Process

Editing can be divided into three major focus areas:
1. message
2. organization
3. mechanics.

In the three stages of editing, each area is addressed separately because it's impossible to pay close attention to all three at the same time. Let's look at the three stages.

Message

Editing should begin with the message because it makes no sense to waste time reorganizing or reviewing the mechanics of text that isn't conveying your points clearly.

To review the clarity of your message, ask yourself a few simple questions. These questions are similar to the ones you asked when you started writing the document (Step 2: Know Where You're Taking Your Readers):

- ◆ Is the purpose or bottom line clear?
- ◆ Is the action required of the reader clear?
- ◆ Are the other important points clear?
- ◆ Is the tone appropriate for the message?
- ◆ Is the message written in a positive (rather than negative) way?

As you answer those questions, mark any text you're not satisfied with (for example, a confusing action step). On a paper copy, circle or highlight a group of words or sentences that may need revision. If you prefer editing only on a screen, use the highlighting feature or put that block of text in a different color.

Go through the entire document, marking places you may revise, before you begin revising. You may want to go through it two or three times. Then work on clarifying your message in each of the places you've marked.

Organization

All documents, even those with just a few paragraphs, need to be organized so that the reader can follow the text easily. The second

STEP 9

stage of editing takes a hard look at how well you've imposed a logical order on the message you're trying to convey.

Here are some questions to ask yourself to determine if your document is properly organized:

- Is information separated into chunks that are easy to digest?
- Are those chunks arranged in a logical sequence?
- Does each paragraph contain just one basic idea so readers won't get confused?
- Are there transitions unifying sentences, paragraphs, and sections to help ideas in the document flow smoothly from start to finish?
- Is the structure reasonably similar throughout different sections?
- Could subheads before key sections make it easier to read?

One method to separate and arrange your ideas is to read the document and list all the key points it conveys. In essence, you're re-outlining it. This is much easier when you're looking at text you've written than it is when you're staring at a blank page. The re-outlining process also will help identify any important concepts that you omitted. You can list them separately at the bottom of the page or on a separate sheet of paper and incorporate them as you reorganize the document. You'll also be able to spot repeated or similar ideas scattered throughout the document and then merge them into a single paragraph or section.

If you developed an initial outline before you started your first draft, compare that version to the re-outline to see if you omitted anything you initially intended to include.

During this stage, you may decide to change the order in which ideas are presented so they flow more logically from one to the next.

Consider adding subheads or a few words before each section (set in bold or italic, perhaps underlined) to pinpoint the key message that follows and to further separate each concept. (See Step 6 for more discussion of subheads.)

Good organization is a more subjective quality than are the message and proper mechanics. For example, the same information can be conveyed through shorter or longer paragraphs. And you can explain a multifaceted concept by using bullets to list the facets or by writing a few traditional paragraphs with no bulleted items.

When you get comfortable with your own method of organizing, you'll find that it not only promotes readability but also simplifies your writing process because you can move text around into separate categories more confidently—and get the document done faster.

Mechanics

Most of the grunt work in editing comes in the third stage: reviewing the mechanics of your text. Mechanics form the micro level of the document, not the macro message or the mid-level organization. Mechanics are the weeds!

Editing for mechanics—spelling, punctuation, grammar, and word usage—may require you to be in a different frame of mind than you are when evaluating message clarity and organization. You need to scrutinize individual words or groups of words instead of the entire document. Here are some questions you need to ask:

- Spelling/typos
  - Are any words misspelled?
  - Are any homonyms (sound-alikes, such as *there* and *their*) used in place of the correct words?
  - Are any words missing or out of place in a sentence?
  - Have you placed apostrophes correctly?
  - Are all proper names spelled correctly?
- Punctuation
  - Do all of your sentences end with appropriate punctuation?
  - Are all commas and periods placed inside quotation marks?
  - Do commas separate all the items in a series?
  - Do semicolons separate all the items in a comma-separated series?

- ◆ Grammar and syntax
  - ◆ Do subjects and verbs agree in number?
  - ◆ Do nouns and pronouns agree in number?
  - ◆ Is text written in a consistent tense?
  - ◆ Are sentences written in a parallel structure?
  - ◆ Are bulleted or numbered lists written in a parallel structure?
  - ◆ Are subheads written in a parallel structure?
  - ◆ Does each introductory phrase directly relate to the noun that immediately follows it?
  - ◆ Is everything written in complete sentences, where appropriate?
  - ◆ Are there short, choppy sentences that can be combined for better flow?
- ◆ Word usage
  - ◆ Is there any stuffy language that can be replaced with simpler words?
  - ◆ Are there any weak passive verbs or verb-nouns that can be replaced with more powerful active verbs?
  - ◆ Can you eliminate any redundant language?
  - ◆ Is there jargon or "business-speak" that can be simplified with more widely understood terminology?

You can start with the spelling/grammar-checking feature usually available with word-processing software. It helps catch obvious mistakes—but *don't* depend on it. The spelling-check feature won't catch homonyms you've used incorrectly (*here, hear; do, due; there, their, they're*); and if you've written *is* when you meant *in*, the software won't catch your mistake. As to the grammar-checking feature, sometimes the software's suggestions are just plain wrong.

Another way to find mistakes is to read your words aloud in a staccato, syllable-by-syllable rhythm so you actually can hear the errors. For example, when sounding out "Lu-pé out-lined four-teen work-flow im-prove-ments is her re-port," you'll probably notice that "is" should be "in." Also try reading the text backward, forcing yourself to review one word at a time instead of getting mesmerized by the flow of sentences and paragraphs.

Editing for mechanics can be handled in many ways. You can print out your document, write your revisions on the paper copy, and then key them into the electronic file. Or you can use the tracking/redlining feature of your word-processing program, which will enable you to keep your original version without interrupting the flow of the newer version. With time, you'll discover the system that works best for you.

Examples of Editing in Action

Editing is partially subjective and always situation-specific. Who your readers are, what your message is, and what you hope to accomplish with your document all affect the finished product. Learning to edit your words is hands-on work, and I wish I could sit with you and make specific suggestions as you do it. Because that's not a viable plan, the second-best option is for you and me to look at several first-draft documents and evaluate their message, organization, and mechanics. Examining those three aspects of each document, choosing what to do to improve them, and seeing how the changes are made will help you learn to edit your own work more effectively.

What follows are three documents: (1) a meeting review, (2) a report on customer service problems, and (3) an explanation of the company purchasing policy. Some of the documents may need correction in one or two of the focus areas; others may need changes in all three areas.

You'll find the rough-draft versions of each document first, followed by an evaluation of the message, the organization, and the mechanics. Because the evaluations are brief and general, you'll gain most from studying the text in "tracked" or redlined format—that is, with deletions, additions, and changes showing. In this format you'll be able to see exactly what was replaced or inserted with a degree of detail that the evaluations don't offer. The tracked version and final ready-to-send version of each document are shown after each evaluation.

Meeting Review

Rough Draft

Carl,

This email is to review and confirm all of the critical and key issues we discussed at the meeting yesterday morning from 9 to 11:00 a.m. In that meeting, we talked about the fact that your staff of employees needs to provide assistance to my team with the different facets of the execution of the direct mail campaign.

Below, I have listed the important next steps, which are bulleted, that need to be followed by your staff:

- *Assuming responsibility for the phone calls to the sources you have in order to be able to build a complete and comprehensive database.*
- *Conducting meetings among your staff and my team in which all personnel present would gain an understanding of what each is responsible for during this entire process.*
- *Handling each and every occasion of complaining by the various customers, many of whom may be displeased with the level and quality of customer service they receive.*
- *How the execution of the database marketing program will proceed, including how much it will cost, what we expect the revenues to be and what type of follow-up we should consider implementing.*

I have all the confidence in the world that both of our teams will work together well to complete all that we need to do and be in a great position to produce an effective direct mail campaign with a lower cost.

Should there be any questions, concerns, or items that you feel should be clarified, please don't hesitate to pick up the phone and call me. Or, if you prefer, you can email me directly.

Sincerely,

Steve

Evaluation

1. **Message:** okay
2. **Organization:** okay
3. **Mechanics:**
   - ◆ weak passive verbs
   - ◆ stuffy language, wordiness
   - ◆ redundancies
   - ◆ non-parallel structure in bulleted items

Editing, in Tracked Format

Carl,

~~This email is to review and~~ **Let's** confirm ~~all of~~ the ~~critical and~~ **key** issues ~~we~~ discussed at ~~the~~ **yesterday's** meeting ~~yesterday morning from 9 to 11:00 a.m. In that meeting, we talked~~ **regarding** ~~about the fact that~~ **the help needed from** your staff ~~of employees needs to provide assistance to my team with the different facets of the execution of~~ **on** the direct mail campaign.

Here are ~~Below, I have listed~~ the ~~important~~ next steps~~, which are bulleted, that need to be followed by~~ **for** your staff:

- **Call your** ~~Assuming responsibility for the phone calls to the~~ sources **to help** ~~you have in order to be able to~~ build a ~~complete and~~ comprehensive database.

- Conduct~~ing~~ meetings **with both of our teams to discuss responsibilities.** ~~among your staff and my team in which all personnel present would gain an understanding of what each is responsible for during this entire process.~~

- Handl**e customer complaints.** ~~ing each and every incidence of complaining by the various s customers, many of whom may be displeased with the level and quality of customer service they receive.~~

- **Determine costs and anticipated revenues.** ~~How the execution of the database marketing program will proceed, including how much it will cost, what we expect the revenues to be and what type of follow-up we should consider implementing.~~

STEP **9**

I'm confident that ~~I have all the confidence in the world that both of~~ our teams will work well together to ~~complete all that we need to do and be in a great position to~~ produce an effective direct mail campaign <u>at</u> ~~with~~ a lower cost.

<u>Please call or email me if you have</u> ~~Should there be~~ any questions~~, concerns, or items that you feel should be clarified, please don't hesitate to pick up the phone and call me. Or, if you prefer, you can email me directly.~~

Sincerely,

Steve

Final Document

Carl,

Let's confirm the key issues discussed at yesterday's meeting regarding the help needed from your staff on the direct mail campaign.

> *Here are the next steps for your staff:*
> - *Call your sources to help build a comprehensive database.*
> - *Conduct meetings with both of our teams to discuss responsibilities.*
> - *Handle customer complaints.*
> - *Determine costs and anticipated revenues.*

> *I'm confident that our teams will work well together to produce an effective direct mail campaign at a lower cost.*

> *Please call or email me if you have any questions.*

Sincerely,

Steve

Report of Customer Service Problems

Rough Draft

Diane,

We in our department always take service very seriously, and believe it's the cornerstone of our business. There's no better in-

dicators of a company's commitment to customers and qualities. Poor service can have a devastating affect on the company. There are also problems in other areas, even with what we thought was a dedicated staff.

Many mistakes have been made on orders. In fact, mistakes have risen 15 percent in the past six months. I suspect this is most likely due to the lack of sufficient understanding of the different products by our customer service representatives. The right training can insure a more positive outcome and go a long way to correcting these mistakes. This should entail expanded training to the tune of 20 hours per month for three months. It's worth it.

Poor service isn't helped by the presence of customer management software that many—including me—consider antiquated. They are contributing to mistakes and making employees frustrated. And we shouldn't neglect the fact that absenteeism among customer service reps is up 25 percent in the past six months. That doesn't work. All employees who have missed five or more workdays in a single month need to meet with you individually. If we have this meeting, invest $75,000 in CMX, the latest customer management package and expand the training as I've indicated, we can improve customer service. Those are some of the issues we face—which obviously need to be dealt with.

Sincerely,

Moises

Evaluation

1. **Message:** garbled. The purpose is not clearly stated in the first paragraph; it is finally alluded to in the second paragraph; and the action step at the end is unclear.
2. **Organization:** poor. The problems (mistakes on orders, old software, and high rate of absenteeism) are scattered throughout the text. Plus, the solution for the outdated software should follow the explanation of the problem.

3. **Mechanics:** poor. Although many of the existing errors will be eliminated when the unnecessary material is deleted and the points are reorganized, it is important to note the current mistakes to avoid:

- redundancies
- wordiness
- errors in subject/verb and noun/pronoun agreement
- poor word usage
- misuse of apostrophe
- points stated negatively instead of positively.

To revise this document, let's first identify the key message: ***Suggested solutions to customer service problems.*** Now let's rewrite it by organizing the information into chunks and deleting redundant language.

Editing, in Tracked Format

Diane,

We <u>have some serious customer service problems that need to be addressed. Below are the three most critical problems and my suggested solutions:</u> ~~in our department always take service very seriously, and believe it's the cornerstone of our business. There's no better indicators of a company's commitment to customers and qualities. Poor service can have a devastating affect on the company. There are also problems in other areas, even with what we thought was a dedicated staff.~~

<u>Problem 1:</u> ~~Many mistakes have been made on orders. In fact, mistakes have risen~~ 15 percent <u>rise in the number of shipping mistakes</u> in the past six months. ~~I suspect this is most likely due to the lack of sufficient understanding of the different products by our customer service representatives. The right training can insure a more positive outcome and go a long way to correcting these mistakes. This should entail~~

<u>Solution:</u> expand~~ed~~ training to ~~the tune of~~ 20 hours ~~per~~ <u>a</u> month for <u>the next</u> three months. ~~It's worth it.~~

Problem 2: ~~Poor service isn't helped by the presence of customer management software that many—including me—consider antiquated. They are contributing to mistakes and making employees frustrated. And we shouldn't neglect the fact that~~ 25 percent rise in absenteeism among customer service reps ~~is up 25 percent~~ in the past six months. ~~That doesn't work.~~

Solution: meet with each ~~All~~ employees who has ~~have~~ missed five or more workdays in a single month. ~~need to meet with you individually.~~

Problem 3: antiquated customer management software.

Solution: ~~If we have this meeting,~~ invest $75,000 in CMX, the latest customer management package. ~~and expand the training as I've indicated, we can improve customer service. Those are some of the issues we face—which obviously need to be dealt with.~~

Sincerely,

Moises

Final Document

Diane,

We have some serious customer service problems that need to be addressed. Below are the three most critical problems and my suggested solutions:

Problem 1: *15 percent rise in the number of shipping mistakes in the past six months.*

Solution: *expand training to 20 hours a month for the next three months.*

Problem 2: *25 percent rise in absenteeism among customer service reps in the past six months.*

Solution: *meet with each employee who has missed five or more workdays in a single month.*

Problem 3: *antiquated customer management software.*

Solution: invest $75,000 in CMX, the latest customer management package.

Sincerely,

Moises

Explanation of Company Purchasing Policy

Rough Draft

So we can do a better job in handling our claims with regard to materials purchased at the MNO or XYZ stores, we are requesting all Contractors to use the supply report for those particular stores. When you use our firm's accounts for these stores, please be absolutely sure that you make a complete purchase for the job at one time. Every time you make a purchase, the store is generating an invoice. As a result, more work is created not only for us, but for you as well.

An example of this occurred when one contractor went to the XYZ store five times in one week for the same claim. Each purchase were for very minor items. This takes time out of your employee's production and project efficiency, as well as costing our firm and you more money for that particular claim.

We've heard many contractors who complain that it takes longer for their employees to relocate the materials at the stores, and this may be the reason why. It's my recommendation that you and your subcontractors email all of the orders into MNO store or XYZ store at least 24 hours prior to the pickup time. Please make sure that you order the materials necessary for a repair job, and have them put it on one invoice. By doing this, we should minimize your employees' and subcontractors down time, travel time, and reduce operating expense for you and our company.

In addition, make certain that you use indicate the correct purchase order number, not the customer's phone number or social security number. If you do not use the correct purchase order number, you will be adviced to go the website of either of the appropriate stores and make all of the corrections for each

claim. This needs to be done. For those of you who continue to have problems with getting the correct purchase order number on the invoices, I will have to take you out of the rotation until this can be corrected.

Evaluation

1. **Message:** fairly clear—procedures for purchases at these stores
2. **Organization:** good
3. **Mechanics:** poor
   - misspelled words
   - redundancies
   - words missing
   - vague use of pronouns, such as *this* and *that,* with no clear noun reference
   - weak passive verbs
   - lack of number agreement between subject and verb
   - stuffy language, wordiness
   - inaccurate capitalization
   - inaccurate use of apostrophe
   - phrases and sentences without parallel structure
   - dangling participle

Editing, in Tracked Format

To ~~So we can do a~~ better ~~job in handling our~~ handle claims for ~~with regard to~~ materials purchased at the MNO or XYZ stores, ~~we are requesting all C~~contractors should ~~to~~ use the supply report for those particular stores. ~~When you use our firm's accounts for these stores, please b~~Be ~~absolutely~~ sure to ~~that you make a complete~~ purchase everything you need for the job at one time. ~~Every time you make a purchase,~~ Otherwise, the store ~~is~~ generat~~es~~ing multiple ~~an~~ invoices for each purchase, resulting in unnecessary work for both of us. ~~As a result, more work is created not only for us, but for you as well.~~

For ~~An~~ example, ~~of this occurred when~~ one contractor went to the XYZ store five times in one week for the same claim, each time.

~~Each purchase were~~ for ~~very~~ minor items. This <u>duplication of effort</u> <u>costs employees valuable production time and</u> ~~takes time out of~~ ~~your employee's production and project efficiency, as well as~~ cost<u>s</u>~~ing~~ ~~our firm~~ <u>the stores</u> ~~and you more money for that particular claim.~~ <u>time and money to produce the extra paperwork.</u>

~~We've heard many contractors who complain that it takes longer for~~ ~~their employees to relocate the materials at the stores, and this may~~ ~~be the reason why. It's my~~ <u>I</u> recommendation ~~that~~ that you and your sub-contractors email all ~~of the~~ orders <u>to</u> ~~into~~ MNO store or XYZ store at least 24 hours prior to the pick-up time<u>, and be.</u> ~~Please make~~ sure that <u>all</u> ~~you order the~~ materials <u>needed for a job are</u> ~~necessary for a~~ ~~repair job, and have them put~~ ~~it~~ <u>listed</u> on one invoice. ~~By doing this,~~ <u>Doing so</u> ~~we~~ should ~~minimize your employees' and subcontractors~~ ~~down time, travel time, and~~ reduce operating expense<u>s</u> for ~~you and~~ ~~our company.~~ <u>all parties.</u>

In addition, <u>remember to submit</u> ~~make certain that you use indi-~~ ~~cate~~ the correct purchase order number, not the customer's phone number or social security number. ~~If you do not use the correct pur-~~ ~~chase order number,~~ <u>Otherwise,</u> you will be <u>forced</u> ~~adviced~~ to go <u>to</u> the website of either ~~of the appropriate~~ store~~s~~ and ~~make all of the~~ correction~~s~~ each claim. ~~This needs to be done. For t~~<u>T</u>hose of you who continue to <u>submit the wrong</u> ~~have problems with getting the cor-~~ ~~rect purchase order~~ numbers on the invoices~~, I~~ will <u>be</u> ~~have to~~ take<u>n</u> ~~you~~ out of the rotation until this <u>error</u> can be corrected.

Final Document

To better handle claims for materials purchased at the MNO or XYZ stores, contractors should use the supply report for those particular stores. Be sure to purchase everything you need for the job at one time. Otherwise, the store generates multiple invoices for each purchase, resulting in unnecessary work for both of us.

For example, one contractor went to XYZ store five times in one week for the same claim, each time for minor items. This duplication of effort costs employees valuable production time and costs the stores time and money to produce the extra paperwork.

I recommend that you and your subcontractors email all orders to MNO store or XYZ store at least 24 hours prior to the pick-up time, and be sure that all materials needed for a job are listed on one invoice. Doing so should reduce operating expenses for all parties.

In addition, remember to submit the correct purchase order number, not the customer's phone number or social security number. Otherwise, you will be forced to go to the website of either store and correct each claim. Those of you who continue to submit the wrong numbers on the invoices will be taken out of the rotation until this error can be corrected.

Your Turn

Editing requires a meticulous review of your document's message (clarity of content), organization (logical structure and flow), and mechanics (punctuation, spelling, grammar, and word usage,). Revise the following document to improve each of those areas. Delete unnecessary words; use simple words and parallel structure; ensure that verbs and subjects agree in number; make verb tense consistent throughout; correct spelling, punctuation, grammar, or usage mistakes; and insert subheads and bullets to improve organization, if desired.

Frank,

Everyone in our division believes strongly in the need for accuracy in shipping. We take it seriously and consider its the part our business that distinguish us from the rest of the competition. Mistakes on orders can be heavily damaging to the company.

Too many errors have occurred on shipments. It has come to my attention that shipment errors have gone up 20 percent over the time period covering the past nine months. It is my opinion that this is probably a result of out dated technology. Thus the only, solution is to make the investment in the latest, state-of-the-art shipping technology. This technology will be so much better for all partys involved.

Nobody likes sloppy work by any one or group. After my observations, I have concluded that a good many of the shipping clerks do work that many, including I, consider sloppy. No way can this be tolerated any more. The entire department needs to undergo training on proper procedures. This training can be handled by PDQ Consultants, experts in this type of training.

We have also notice a large number of safety violations, that can be dangerous if they're not corrected. So let's get on it. I want those violations to be corrected within a four-month time period. The best ones to handle this is RL Risk Services, an excellent risk management firm. Let's get on this.

Regards,

Bob

The Next Step

Most of us write specific types of documents more often than others. To become proficient at applying all the skills described in this book to the communications we produce most frequently, it's good to master those types of documents. We'll take a closer look at doing that in Step 10: Master the Documents You Use Most Often.

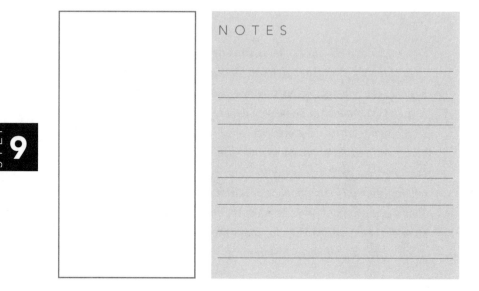

NOTES

STEP 9

Master the Documents You Use Most Often

OVERVIEW

Comprehensive instructions for writing

- Email
- Performance reviews
- Business proposals
- Client activity reports
- Audit reports
- Letters to a customer
- PowerPoint slides
- Press releases

Although the writing skills addressed in this book can be applied to practically every type of business document, you should develop techniques to improve the quality of those you write frequently. This step explains the strategies for writing several different documents, and it includes examples of each type.

Email

An email really isn't a type of document; it's simply a means to deliver your message. But the explosion of email communication in the past decade has focused much attention on email efficiency. According to a recent survey by Cohesive Information Solutions (www.cohesivesolutions.com), working professionals spend 40 percent of their time reading, writing, and interpreting emails. Here's the scary part: a third of that time is wasted—an amount of time that, extrapolated, translates to $308 billion in lost productivity each year! Clearly, there is a great need for help in writing emails.

To be a more efficient and professional email communicator, treat emails like any other business document. Don't cheat on grammar. Don't use funky fonts or symbols such as happy faces. Don't use abbreviations that only the teen text-messaging crowd understands. And write text that's concise and well organized so readers can quickly grasp your message.

Craft Explicit Subject Lines

Email subject lines are like newspaper headlines. Just as we select articles to read on the basis of their headlines, we choose which emails to read largely on the basis of subject lines. To get your email read sooner than someone else's email—or to get it read at all—write more explicit subject lines.

Here's a little test of this point. Which email subject line in each of these pairs would you open first?

1a. March shipping report
 b. Action needed: March shipping errors up 20%

2a. First-quarter profitability
 b. First-quarter profitability up 12%

3a. XY Industries feedback
 b. XY Industries upset: wants conference call this week

Be Brief, Be Organized

Below are some suggestions for writing concise, organized email text and samples that show the suggestions in action. You'll recognize these tips from earlier steps because they apply to many types of documents.

1. Start by explaining your purpose for writing and what you want readers to do:

We need to submit the marketing budget by June 1, so please review the costs listed below and email me any additions or changes by May 15.

POINTER Write explicit subject lines for your email so recipients will open them quickly.

2. Use bullets wherever you can to simplify the message. Be sure to give your bullet points parallel structure:

   The division manager said our team needs to improve in these areas:

   ◆ *faster response to customer inquiries*

   ◆ *fewer errors on orders to overseas clients*

   ◆ *more accurate budget reports.*

3. Use subheads to separate categories of information:

   Below are my suggestions for promoting our latest software:

   INTERNET ADS

   Place banner ads on the top niche-industry websites.

   FLASH EMAILS

   Send flash emails to the 5,000 clients and prospects listed in the nationwide database.

   PRESS RELEASES

   Distribute press releases highlighting the software's benefits to small employers.

   Note the use of all-caps type for the subheads but not for the regular text. Typing the body of the message in all caps would indicate "shouting."

Performance Review

If you were asked by a senior executive to summarize one of your subordinates' performances, your reply might go something like this: *Ning Lee is a hard-working account executive who has a great rapport with customers, but he makes too many reporting errors and needs to be a better team player.*

Consider starting a review with exactly that kind of a big-picture approach that summarizes the person's strengths, challenges, overall

STEP **10**

performance during the past 6 or 12 months, and your recommendations. For more negative reviews, however, you may not want to put too much bad news up front.

Some companies require you to follow a performance review template and answer specific questions, which can make it difficult to describe certain aspects of the employee's accomplishments or shortcomings. In those cases, see if you can add that introductory paragraph to sum up the individual's performance.

See example 10.1 for two suggested outline options you can use to write performance reviews. Sometimes these outlines can be modified to fit a company's template. Naturally, the categories listed would change according to the position being reviewed.

The sample performance review presented in example 10.2 uses the first outline option. Notice how the first paragraph sums up the employee's performance over the past 12 months.

Business Proposal

The most important part of any proposal (whether for new business, for a new initiative, or for any other desired outcome), is the beginning. Start with a convincing argument for why the reader should buy into your ideas. In the case of new business proposals, your argument should distinguish you and your company from others who might be competing for the same account.

EXAMPLE 10.1

Sample Outlines for Performance Reviews— Two Options

Option 1

- *Overview:* big picture in two or three sentences
- *Strengths* (goals met or exceeded):
  - phone skills
  - product knowledge
  - working with team
- *Challenges* (goals not met):
  - phone skills
  - product knowledge
  - working with team
- *Recommendations:* probation, training, promotion, and so forth

Option 2

- *Overview:* big picture in two or three sentences
- *Product knowledge:*
  - strengths
  - challenges
- *Phone skills:*
  - strengths
  - challenges
- *Working with team:*
  - strengths
  - challenges
- *Recommendations:* probation, training, promotion, and so forth

If you start with a paragraph that explains your idea in a nutshell, your reader should be able to spare at least a few minutes to read those first few sentences and, we hope, will be enticed to read more. You also should write a compelling title—a task that's often easier to do after you've written the first paragraph.

The rest of the proposal should address specifics of the concepts mentioned in the overview, other information that will promote your company and its products or services, and whatever else the prospective

EXAMPLE 10.2

Sample Performance Review Using Option 2

Employee: Lucinda Torres, account manager

Performance period: November 15, 2006, to November 15, 2007

Overview

A hard-working account executive, Lucinda Torres, consistently handles more phone calls than required and scores high on customer service. Lucinda has demonstrated an ability to grasp personal lines products, but she hasn't shown the same understanding of commercial lines products. To be promoted to the next level, Lucinda needs to improve her commercial lines knowledge and spend more time helping colleagues to show that she's a team player.

Product knowledge

◆ Strengths

Having eight years' experience with auto, home, and fire insurance, Lucinda has an intimate knowledge of all personal lines products, and has learned the new provisions as they've been introduced.

◆ Challenges

Lucinda has struggled sometimes to understand commercial lines because she lacks experience with these products. The few customer complaints against her have concerned commercial lines. She needs to spend more time learning these policies.

Phone skills

◆ Strengths

Over the past 12 months, Lucinda has handled an average of 15 percent more calls than required for her position. Plus, her customer service rating has been 8 of 10 or higher for the entire period. In that time, only three official customer complaints have been filed against her, the lowest number received for any member of the team.

- Challenges

  The only area in which Lucinda needs to improve is explaining commercial lines products. She often speaks too quickly to customers—perhaps to hide her uncertainty—and some people have called to request clarification.

Working with team

- Strengths

  Many less-experienced account managers have a better grasp of personal lines policies as a result of Lucinda's workshops and the time she spends answering their questions.

- Challenges

  Lucinda tends to help others on her team only when asked. She should be reaching out to other account managers more often, letting them know she's available to help. Given her extensive product knowledge, she could be a far greater asset to the rest of the team.

Recommendations

Lucinda Torres, who has proven to be an asset to the team, could be ready for a promotion within the next six months. Over the next three months, she should complete the team dynamics course, which can teach her the keys to working better with team members. Plus, she should attend the weekly sales meeting whenever a new commercial lines product is introduced. If Lucinda demonstrates significant improvement as a team player in commercial lines after completing these steps, she should be promoted to senior account executive.

STEP 10

client is expecting. All this information should be presented in a logical sequence. These sections could comprise the objectives, target audiences, strategies, fees, and more about your firm (see example 10.3 for a sample proposal).

Client Activity Report

Most clients want to know if what you've done for them is worth what they're paying you, so you submit a client activity report at certain predetermined times. This activity report describes your actions on behalf of your client—what you've done for the money you or your organization is getting. The report should be a combination of descriptive text, ideally in short paragraphs, and bulleted or numbered lists of specific action items or recommendations. Use subheads to separate the sections of the report to focus your reader's attention on the individual details of the report. Example 10.4 offers a brief activity report as a sample.

Audit Report

An effective audit report should first state the purpose of the audit and the most pertinent conclusions, thus immediately conveying the general result of the audit. Then the report should explain all facets of the audit in a logical sequence and with details of the process. The report also may include lists, such as people interviewed, key observations, and the supporting documents attached. The product-specific audit for a contract supplier presented in example 10.5 suggests specific sections that might be applicable to audits in your organization. As with so much other business communication, it's vital that you separate your specific topics into clearly organized paragraphs and that you define those topics with descriptive subheads.

EXAMPLE 10.3

New Business Proposal

Powerful, consistent messages to build the Iowa Association of Working Professionals (AWP) brand:

I. Overview: Consistent Messages to Build Visibility

The Iowa Association of Working Professionals (AWP) plays a critical role for working professionals and offers outstanding value to its members—but many don't know this. The association needs to drive this message home to members, prospects, legislators, and other key audiences. Doing so will help engage members and recruit new ones.

SG Communications, with extensive experience in association communication, can craft the various elements of this message. These elements would include how membership benefits the bottom line, how AWP's legislative initiatives help members succeed, how AWP's educational programs improve management functions, and how networking at AWP generates new business leads.

II. Objectives

- *Build AWP's brand as the voice of the industry.*
- *Help recruit more members.*
- *Demonstrate the value of AWP membership, such as educational programs, a voice at the state capital, updates on industry trends, and discounts on various services.*
- *Support AWP's legislative agenda.*

III. Target Audiences

- *Current and prospective AWP members*
- *Key legislators*

continued on next page

Example 10.3, continued

◆ Other key Iowa business leaders and organizations

◆ Key Iowa media

IV. **Strategy: Reshape Messages to Address "What's in It for Me?"**

The key to achieving the objectives is crafting clear and powerful messages that convey the value that AWP offers. SG will work with AWP to reshape messages so they speak directly to the audience's needs. Although AWP has been promoting member benefits for many years, its messages to explain them need to better answer the question, "What's in it for me?"

Among the potential messages:

◆ *AWP's programs help you improve management skills and grow your business.*

◆ *AWP's member benefits, including shipping discounts, offer bottom-line savings.*

◆ *AWP's job retraining programs serve an essential role in the business community.*

V. **Tactics: Deliver Consistent Messages through Many Vehicles**

To deliver its messages effectively, AWP should incorporate several tactics—which could include print and e-newsletters, broadcast faxes, publicity, and a revamped website. All of these vehicles would work together to deliver the association's messages consistently.

VI. **Fee**

$72,000 for a 12-month program, billed at $6,000 a month. The fee covers research; concept development; client contact; writing, editing, and revising of documents.

VII. **About SG Communications, LLC**

Founded in 1997, SG Communications offers public relations, marketing communications, and business writing instruction. Our team of experienced professionals can provide the solutions you need. Whether it's a proactive publicity program, a public affairs campaign, a compelling newsletter, or a workshop to improve business writing skills, SG can deliver the desired results.

EXAMPLE 10.4

Client Activity Report

Fogart Environmental Consulting Media Placement Report

Submitted by SG Communications, LLC

Overview

Over the past three months, SG Communications has secured a steady flow of articles on Fogart Environmental Consulting's major projects and on key issues such as the proposed changes in environmental regulations. Three of these stories prompted letters to the editor from small business owners, a clear indication that the public is paying attention to Fogart's positions. As a result, Tom Fogart, company president, is being recognized as one of Texas's leading environmental experts.

Articles: April to June

- *Dallas Morning News, April. 7*: Front-page story on new state environmental regulations, quoting Tom
- *Austin American-Statesman, May 17*: Article in business section on Fogart Environmental Consulting's contract with several municipalities in Austin metropolitan area
- *Waco Tribune-Herald, June 2*: Tom's opinion-editorial column suggesting new federal environmental guidelines
- *San Antonio Standard-Times, June 20*: Article on new trends in environmental industry, quoting Tom.
- *Odessa American*: Profile on Fogart Environmental Consulting in conjunction with the firm's 15th anniversary

Next Steps

- *Continue proactive media contact, suggesting stories on other topics, including those that affect specific regions in Texas.*
- *Begin planning conference for October or November where Tom Fogart would lead a panel of experts to explore Texas's most pressing environmental issues.*
- *Develop a survey on the effectiveness of new state environmental regulations; distribute survey to employers in targeted Texas cities; and, after analyzing respondent data, write and issue press release.*

EXAMPLE 10.5

External Audit Report

External Audit: XY Company's Qualifications as Packaging Operation for Product Z

Purpose

This audit was conducted to assess the capability of XY Company to perform labeling, secondary packaging, and distribution of Product Z, especially regarding the control of supplies from start to finish.

Conclusion

XY Company is qualified to perform labeling, secondary packaging, and distribution of Product Z.

General Methods

A three-person team conducted the audit through conference room discussions, interviews with employees, and reviews of selected documentation in relevant areas.

Location

The audit was conducted at the XY Company's Portland, Maine, facility, a 110,000-square-foot building devoted to primary and secondary blister packaging.

Summary of Findings

- *The packaging areas were neat, clean, and well-organized, which promoted a smooth, well-run operation.*
- *The receiving area was congested because of the high volume of material received.*

Specific Findings

1. Receipt and storage areas:

Materials received are hand-recorded on receiving documents, transferred to a computerized Access QAD (Quality Inventory System), and inspected. XY Company is constructing a self-contained sampling booth for raw materials. Once checked, the materials are moved to a staging corridor and held until ready for processing. The corridor was well organized, except for a few partially broken pallets not properly aligned in the racks.

Observation A: One end of each storage rack is identified by a number (for example, C203) and the other end is identified with the same number. The pallet spaces between are designated C203A, C203B, C203C, and so forth, but are not labeled as such. That could result in an improper pallet being pulled from the racks.

Observation B: Package inserts are commingled in the storage area with general packaging materials, a procedure not recognized as an industry standard.

2. Manufacturing, in-process storage, and warehouse areas:

The manufacturing areas were neat and clean, efficient, and optimized for workflow. The movement of materials was well orchestrated and performed in a manner that suggested it was well controlled. The primary packaging areas were self-contained and meticulously clean. Because of space constraints, finished products were staged in the warehouse area and then moved to the offsite warehouse, where they awaited final disposition.

Recommendations

* Maintain a person in the plant during all packaging operations.
* Review and sign master packaging record.
* Review and accept each batch production record.
* Review and accept all deviations that may occur during packaging.

Letter to a Customer

Keeping clients happy—or at least less angry—is essential to most businesses. Unless all aspects of your company are perfect, customers will get upset from time to time—perhaps because they've bought a defective product from you, they've been charged an amount they don't think is justified, your customer service reps haven't returned their calls or emails, or there was a delay in promised service. It doesn't matter if these problems are real or perceived; the customer must be calmed and satisfied if her or his relationship with your company is going to continue. The way you reply to a customer who contacts you—either with complaints or praise—will make a huge difference in how your organization is perceived among buyers in the marketplace. (See Step 7 for more about categorizing your relationship with your customer and about setting the right tone in your message.)

Here are some tips to use when writing to a customer (either by email or snail mail).

◆ If your firm has made a mistake, admit it without making excuses.

◆ Address the customer's specific complaint instead of offering a canned response crafted for use in all similar situations.

◆ If the customer is wrong, don't insult his or her intelligence or motives. Point out how the person could have thought he or she was right and the company was wrong. Acknowledge that no company is ever perfect (no matter how hard it tries), and carefully point out the facts of the disputed matter.

◆ Don't patronize the customer with trite language such as, "At ABC Company, we love every one of our loyal customers."

◆ Empathize with the customer, putting yourself in that person's shoes when, for example, he or she was

> **POINTER**
> Offer to go the extra mile—do some research for the customer or offer credit toward the next purchase.

inconvenienced by delivery of the wrong product or untimely response to service problems.

◆ Invite the customer to call *you*—through a direct line—if she or he has additional questions or concerns.

◆ Where possible, offer to go the extra mile—do some research for the customer or offer some credit toward the next purchase. When you do this in a supportive, concerned manner, the value to the customer will far exceed the cost to the company—and will repair/strengthen the relationship between the two parties.

> **POINTER**
>
> Address the customer's complaint specifically and avoid canned replies.

There's a sample letter in example 10.6. Let's review that letter to see how we applied some of those tips:

◆ Address the specific complaint and empathize with your customer:

> *What a disappointment it must have been to find that your health insurance premium was $300 a month more than you anticipated.*
>
> *We know how expensive employee benefits can be, especially for a small business owner like you.*

◆ Don't insult your customer's intelligence if his or her complaint is not supported by the facts:

> *Though the spreadsheet we sent you showed the figures accurately, we understand how you could have mistaken the parent and child premium for the family premium. Several other clients have been confused by our rate sheet, and we're working on revising the layout so it's easier to understand.*

◆ Where possible, offer to go the extra mile:

> *What we can do is take another look at your entire employee benefits program to see if there are other ways we could lower your costs.*

STEP 10

EXAMPLE 10.6

Letter to a Customer

Dear Ms. Rosner:

*What a disappointment it must have been to find that your health insurance premium was $300 a month more than you anticipated. To cover your husband and two children, you need the **family rate** and not the less-costly **parent-and-child rate.***

Though the spreadsheet we sent you showed the figures accurately, we understand how you could have mistaken the parent-and-child premium for the family premium. Several other clients have been confused by our rate sheet, and we're working on revising the layout so it's easier to understand.

We know how expensive employee benefits can be, especially for a small business owner like you. Unfortunately, health insurance premiums for employers with 2 to 50 workers are set by the state insurance department, and we have no control over them. We wish we did.

What we can do is take another look at your entire employee benefits program to see if there are other ways we could lower your costs. I'll call you next week to discuss the possibilities. Meanwhile, please feel free to call me at 203.555.6349.

Sincerely,

Latisha Coates, Senior Account Manager

◆ Invite the customer to call you by a direct number:

> *Meanwhile, please feel free to call me at 203.555.6349.*

As you can see from that example, a lot of ground can be covered in a short letter—and a relationship can be saved and cemented.

PowerPoint Slides

Like other forms of technology-assisted communication, Microsoft PowerPoint is a great tool that's often misused. Too many speakers use PowerPoint as a crutch, making the slides—rather than them-

POINTER

Use Microsoft PowerPoint slides to keep the audience focused on what you're saying.

selves—the focus of their presentations. Some presenters try to write most or all of what they plan to say directly on the slides—and then they read it to the audience. There's nothing more boring than a speaker reading his or her presentation off a screen.

Use slides as your speaking outline to keep yourself on track and as focus points to keep your audience centered on what you're saying. Your slides many carry only words, a combination of words and visuals (photos, clip art, illustrations, charts, diagrams, and tables), or visuals alone. See tool 10.1 for the dos and don'ts of slide making.

Compare the following three pairs of PowerPoint slides. The first entry in each pair is too word heavy; the second entry shows you how to pare down the text to hit the memorable points.

1. **Wordy:**

   ### *Marketing Objectives*

   ◆ *We need to achieve a 15 percent higher market share in the southwest region.*

   ◆ *We should be able to generate 500 more leads by targeting the telecommunications sector.*

   ◆ *We can expand our reach to two key cities, Santa Fe and Tucson.*

   Concise:

   ### *Marketing Objectives*

   ◆ *15% more market share*

   ◆ *500 more leads in telecom sector*

   ◆ *Expansion to Santa Fe & Tucson*

2. **Wordy:**

   ### *Tactics*

   ◆ *Produce and distribute e-newsletters for the entire database of clients and prospects.*

   ◆ *Place print ads in the Sunday newspapers of all key cities in our target market.*

◆ *Develop banner ads to post on key websites read by those in the telecommunications industry.*

Concise:

Tactics

◆ *E-newsletters: clients and prospects*

◆ *Print ads: Sunday papers*

◆ *Banner ads: telecom sites*

3. **Wordy:**

Next Steps

A. *Arrange for a brainstorming session to help develop key concepts to deliver our messages.*

TOOL 10.1

Tips for Making Microsoft PowerPoint Slides Most Effective

◆ Use phrases instead of sentences, and don't bother about periods at the ends.

◆ Omit short words like the, in, of, and so on.

◆ Abbreviate and use dashes, colons, and slashes, and ampersands to save space.

◆ Use a consistent, parallel structure within each slide—for example, make each line on a slide a command or a question.

◆ Frequently use bullets or numerals to group items.

◆ Don't clutter a slide with too much information.

◆ Write no more than six or seven lines on any slide.

◆ For headlines, use 36-point type or larger; for text, use 24-point type or larger.

◆ Stick to one or two typefaces.

◆ Minimize the amount of text you put in all caps because it's more difficult to read.

◆ To break up a presentation that's full of text-heavy slides, throw in a few slides that have only visuals to represent a concept you can discuss.

◆ Use color combinations with sharp contrasts, like blue and yellow.

◆ Before your audience arrives, go to the back of the room and view the slides to ensure that they can be read easily from there.

B. *Instruct creative team to develop three ad campaigns to present to us for evaluation.*

   C. *Select the best one of those campaigns and fine-tune the ideas.*

   D. *Have creative team produce two versions of the ad for the trade and consumer audiences.*

Concise:

   Next Steps

   A. *Brainstorm ad concepts*

   B. *Develop 3 campaigns*

   C. *Select/fine-tune best one*

   D. *Develop 2 ads: trade & consumer*

Press Release

Newspaper, magazine, and website editors and TV/radio producers are swamped with press releases—and so many of the releases are completely irrelevant to their audiences. Other releases are somewhat related to the readers, viewers, or listeners but offer nothing more than pure hype. Still other releases that have some news value are blandly titled, badly organized, or much too long. The winners that rise to the top in the tangle of press releases submitted to news outlets are the concise, organized, and well-written messages that convey their major news in the lead and that flesh out the story in brief paragraphs arranged in an order of descending importance. (Remember what I said about editors cutting from the bottom?)

Among the small number of press releases in that last category—those that get to the point right away and grab the editor's or producer's attention—only a few are considered for use as a short piece or a feature or are put on the backburner for a future story. That's how challenging it is to write releases that break through to the media.

To appreciate why getting editors or producers to read your releases is so difficult, picture a scene that occurs every morning in

STEP **10**

newsrooms and offices nationwide. A harried, stressed-out editor at her desk is skimming hundreds of emails from public relations agencies or people representing businesses and affinity groups of all sizes, corporations, nonprofits, municipalities, political candidates, and other individuals or entities hoping to grab the public eye or ear at no cost. The decision to open or delete an email is based on how well the editor knows the source and how effectively the headline (in the subject line) piques her interest. If the editor opens the email, the lead better be compelling enough to hold her interest beyond 30 seconds. The headline and lead in an ink-and-paper release (for example, as part of a press kit) have to pack the same power to intrigue. As one editor told me, "If the copy doesn't excite me in the first 20 words, I won't read the rest of it." And he wasn't kidding.

POINTER

In a press release, craft a headline and a brief lead sentence or paragraph that breaks through a news editor's mailbox clutter.

To write gripping headlines and leads, you need to look beyond the obvious facts about your product, service, event, or issue and uncover its most significant news value. Let's look at some techniques for creating newsworthy headlines and leads.

Compelling Headlines/ Subject Lines

One way to develop legitimate news angles is to visualize how that story would come across in a particular newspaper or magazine or on a radio or TV broadcast. Then craft a headline (also the subject line of an emailed release) that grabs attention and a lead paragraph that concisely conveys your news. Compare these two headlines:

1. *XY Group's first-quarter profits increase 5% as CEO cites "new opportunities" for growth*
2. *XY Group's 5% hike in profits means 900 new hires by July 1*

The second headline not only conveys the rise in profits, but also the impact of that rise on the community—900 new hires. This would be especially appealing to a regional business editor or producer interested in local employment.

Leads That Summarize Your Principal News

Whereas the headline grabs attention and sometimes actually conveys news (as in the headline example above), the lead (that is, the first paragraph) summarizes the primary news. Compare these two leads:

1. *A new, state-of-the-art database management software program is now available from HZ Technologies, according to an announcement made today. The software uses revolutionary data-mining technology developed after years of research by HZ's R&D team. The software, developed to meet the needs of small businesses, permits the tracking of leads five times faster than previous packages.*

2. *HZ Technologies' new database management software enables small businesses to track leads five times faster than previous packages.*

That first lead uses clichés like "state-of-the-art" and "revolutionary"—turnoffs to editors tired of reading fluff. Plus, the most important news—faster lead tracking—isn't mentioned until the third sentence. By that time, most editors and producers have moved on to the next release.

The second lead gets to the point much faster. In one sentence, it explains the software's benefit to small businesses—and it does that without over-the-top language.

The body of the press release should build on the message in the headline and lead. Using the example of HZ Technologies, the next few paragraphs should explain why the software was developed, how it works, and how other small businesses have used it successfully. The release also could include quotes from an HZ Technologies' executive and from a satisfied client.

Example 10.7 is a press release for a paint manufacturer, written to highlight the manufacturer's new color selection tools. Take a few minutes to read it carefully and then come back to the following review of its contents.

STEP **10**

EXAMPLE 10.7

Press Release

[Headline/Subject line]
Muralo Paints' New "Color Fashions" Ease Color Selection to Help Achieve Ideal Look

[Lead]
Bayonne, NJ, Aug. 1—Muralo Paints has introduced a new "Color Fashions" program featuring a palette of 304 contemporary colors and sophisticated selection tools that allow consumers and designers to easily visualize and test different color combinations. Tools include single-color chips, large color sheets, and tintable samples.

[Second paragraph]
The Color Fashions system features a user-friendly rack with 2.5" x 5.25" single-color chips laid out so people easily can envision different color combinations. The large 7.5" x 11" color sheets and "color tester" quart-size cans—tintable to any color in four different bases—enable homeowners and designers to examine how colors appear in various lights and with different furniture and fabric.

[Quote from company executive]
"It's never been easier to capture the right colors," says Peter Seaborg, Muralo's vice president of sales. "Most consumers don't want to sort through a confusing combination of 1,000 or 1,500 colors." The 304 new colors are the ones most desired by designers and homeowners, according to Seaborg. Muralo always has developed products to meet customer demand—such as Ultra Ceramic, the first flat, scrubbable interior paint, introduced in 2002.

About Muralo

[Boilerplate information]
The Muralo Company, headquartered in Bayonne, New Jersey, produces some of the finest interior and exterior paints, primers, and coatings in the world. One division, Elder & Jenks, is the oldest continuously operating brush and roller maker in the United States, having opened its doors in 1793. Today, Muralo employs more than 200 people. For more information, call 800-631-3440 or visit www.muralo.com.

[Media contact]
Jack E. Appleman, SG Communications, 845.782.2419, appleman@yahoo.com

◆ **Headline/subject line conveys the news:** "Color Fashions" selection system makes it easy to choose the right colors and to achieve the ideal look

◆ **Lead (first paragraph) explains the key selling point:** new system features 304 new colors and enables users to visualize and test color combinations easily

◆ **Second paragraph goes into greater detail:** describes the selection tools—user-friendly rack, large color sheets, and tintable samples

◆ **Quote from company executive personalizes the message and puts a face/voice to the company:** explains the problem to which the company has produced a solution— the confusion of selecting colors

◆ **Boilerplate information offers standard information about the company:** describes the history and structure of the organization

◆ **Contact information makes it easy to reach you:** tells the editor or producer how to get in touch with you for additional details or to develop a more comprehensive treatment of your news.

Your Turn

In addition to practicing the key writing skills needed, you should pay special attention to the types of documents you frequently write. Choose and complete those exercises below that suit your needs most closely.

1. Today, the vast majority of documents are sent through email. Get readers to open your emails sooner by writing compelling and explicit subject lines. Write subject lines that would encourage readers to open each of the following email messages:

   ◆ **To a supervisor:** *I've been thinking about how to lower the costs of computers, printers, scanners, and other equipment. After reviewing an itemized list of purchases over the past 12 months, I see that these items are* bought only when new employees are hired or when an old machine breaks down. That is not cost efficient because we're not getting any volume discounts purchasing one item at a time. I suggest that division managers better anticipate when new personnel will be hired so several machines can be bought at once and we can save as much as 20 percent on purchases throughout the year.

◆ **To peers:** *We've come to that point of the year when we need to hire temporary bookkeepers. In the past three years, this hiring has been a near-disaster. All three temp agencies have assigned inexperienced bookkeepers, and we have wasted so much time explaining basic facts about financials. The obvious solution would be to demand more experienced bookkeepers, but that might blow our budget. Any ideas? Please email your thoughts.*

◆ **To subordinates:** *I'm getting too many complaints from the senior managers at Haz Construction Management, one of our most important clients, about the support staff's "abrasiveness." I know Haz's managers aren't the easiest people to deal with, but we need to keep them happy. Before I tell all of you how to change your behavior, I'd like to hear suggestions from you on how we as a team can change our procedures or approach to make this relationship more pleasant for everyone involved. Please email me your thoughts by January 31, and then we'll meet to fine-tune the ideas.*

2. A new business proposal that immediately explains the key selling point can engage the prospect, encouraging him or her to read more. That's why an executive summary—which conveys the main concept in one or two paragraphs—can help close the sale. Find a proposal that your company recently developed and write a one-paragraph executive summary that concisely explains the ideas contained in the proposal.

3. Many presenters create PowerPoint slides with too much text and then read the text to the audience. A better plan is to use the slides as an outline for the oral presentation. Text should be as brief as possible and need not be written in complete sentences. Below is the material to be covered on three slides. Rewrite the text so that each bullet point is no more than six words. And remember to make the contents of each slide parallel in structure.

A. *Lowering travel expenses:*
   - *We've got a problem in that travel expenses have risen 35% in the past 6 months.*
   - *If we begin holding videoconferences every other month, we won't have to visit clients every single month.*
   - *According to my calculations, our division would reduce travel expenses by $50,000 over the next 6 months.*

B. *Reducing absenteeism:*
   - *I've noticed that absenteeism has risen 20% since our reorganization just over two years ago.*
   - *Part of the problem is poor morale, which we've ignored for far too long.*
   - *My idea is to hold individual meetings with each employee to determine the problem.*

C. *New sales office in Phoenix:*
   - *There are great opportunities to generate sales in the Phoenix area, with its growing population.*
   - *The cost to open this office would be $250,000, which includes salaries of the 10 new people to be hired.*
   - *Our initial projections show that we could generate $500,000 in sales within the first 9 months.*

4. Working from the facts below (listed in random order), write the headline and lead for a press release describing a new stock-picking software. Change the wording to make it more compelling and to convey news value to editors and producers.

STEP 10

◆ The recent credit problem is sending shock waves through the stock markets.

◆ With this volatility, there are outstanding opportunities for short-term traders.

◆ The new *Sacord Predictions* software, unveiled October 1, produces a short list of stocks to watch as the market opens every trading day.

◆ *Sacord Predictions* was developed by Sacord-Tico Investing of Altoona, PA.

◆ The picks are based on key growth and momentum criteria that *Sacord Predictions* can identify.

◆ Studies have shown that *Sacord Predictions* can deliver substantial one-day gains.

◆ *Sacord Predictions* updates itself automatically, including the latest market data.

◆ The software is able to scan the market quickly for the best picks, at user-selected intervals throughout day.

◆ A six-month license for *Sacord Predictions* can be purchased online or on CD-Rom for $275.

N O T E S

APPENDIX

Steps to Improve Workers' Writing Skills

If you're responsible for performance at your company or organization—or if you have some stake in getting employees to work more productively—pay attention to the overall quality of writing. As discussed in the introduction to *10 Steps to Successful Business Writing,* poor writing hurts the bottom line and better writing boosts productivity and delivers other benefits.

Follow these steps to improve the quality of writing at your company:

1. Decide if there is a lack of writing skills among employees.
2. Identify employees who need the most help.
3. Get senior management's buy-in for a writing training program.
4. Choose the best learning method(s) to use with your employees.
5. Design a writing training program.
6. Follow up to maximize results.
7. Create a corporate culture that stresses good writing.
8. Link good writing to leadership and advancement.
9. Establish company writing style standards.
10. Encourage submissions to company publications.
11. Stress straightforward language for employees whose first language is not English.

Decide That There Is a Lack of Writing Skills Among Employees

People in different positions and departments throughout your company may realize that the quality of writing among the employees isn't where it should be. Those critics may include the head of the training or HR department, one of the principals, or some other worker who just can't bear to read another incomprehensible document. There may be complaints from workers who are confused by vague instructions from their supervisors or whose productivity is compromised by miscommunication with other departments. Worse, you may get complaints for customers who say the letters they receive are incoherent, have embarrassingly poor grammar or obvious typos, or are insensitive to their needs.

As a result of any one or more of those prompts, the word gets to someone with the authority to take action—and efforts are begun to raise the quality of the written communication in your organization.

When concern or complaints move the firm to take steps to improve its employees' writing skills, you have to find out specifically where the problem is and which employees need the most help.

POINTER

Some top executives write poorly and some workers at lower levels write well. Don't make any uninformed assumptions when assessing individuals' writing skills.

Identify Employees Who Need the Most Help

Which categories of employees struggle most with their writing? If you assume that senior employees write better than mid- and lower-level employees, you may be wrong. If you think that those in leadership positions have a command of the written word, again you may be surprised. I know of no statistics that pinpoint which employees—whether categorized by experience, position, age, or other criteria—are the most or least competent writers of business documents.

Many senior executives have risen through the ranks with mediocre or poor writing ability, partly because the business community traditionally has not stressed the importance of writing. Skills such as generating leads, closing deals, and managing others have catapulted many workers to the top of the organization chart, with little notice taken of their ability to communicate effectively in writing. Secretaries and executive assistants have carried the communication water for many of these highly compensated employees. Entry-level employees usually are not told that writing will be an important criterion for advancement, and most workers haven't had any writing instruction since high school or college.

Here are some of the best ways to identify those employees who need to improve their writing:

- Email people in key positions (HR/learning directors, division heads, managers, for example) and ask them to assess their subordinates' writing skills. Or ask them to submit sample documents (with proprietary information crossed out, if necessary) so that you can judge employees' writing skills. Depending on the number of samples you receive, establish a team of people to review the documents and identify those workers who would benefit from writing training.
- Either face-to-face or via email, ask top executives if they believe improving their writing could help them work more productively.
- In the company newsletter, on the intranet, or by other means, publish or circulate news about the company's initiative to improve employee writing skills. Provide contact information workers can use to learn more about the training offered.
- If your firm sends out customer surveys, include a section that asks for an evaluation of the correspondence the customers receive from the company. Ask customers to rate such measures as clarity, organization, and empathy.

Many employees will jump at the chance to improve their writing. Others may be offended that they were singled out as poor writers who need help. Supervisors should approach those subordinates who have been singled out and speak with them about enrolling in the training, describing the training not as a punishment but as an opportunity that not all employees get. Explain to those workers who are designated to take the course that virtually every person in the company could benefit from this type of training, and they've been selected because of the importance of the documents they write. All of that is true.

Get Senior Management's Buy-in for a Writing Training Program

Many owners or executives who authorize spending are leery of allocating dollars to improve skills that can't be tied directly to increased revenues. There are so many more tangible items to invest in, they argue—especially efforts that can produce more sales.

The challenge is convincing the check-signers that an investment in writing training will pay off. And if you're a principal of a large or small company, you may have a tough time convincing yourself that training people to write well is worth the time and money needed. Well, here's a simple and convincing truth: *employees who don't write well waste time, and that wastes money.*

If management insists, can you quantify this pre-training waste of time and then project the difference after a writing training program? Yes. Develop a quantitative matrix that analyzes the number of hours spent writing and rewriting documents, the time that could be saved, and the fewer dollars that could be lost. In the best case, simply pointing out that "poor writing hurts the company and better writing helps the company" will be convincing. If the person clutching the purse strings doesn't buy into that premise, he or she may not ever be convinced by a complex quantitative analysis. For those of you who must crunch numbers to get the buy-in, good luck. The good news is that, in recent years, many companies have begun to recognize how investing in improving writing skills will pay dividends.

Choose the Best Learning Method(s) for Your Employees

Today there are more learning options than ever, including traditional classroom, videoconferencing, e-learning and programs on CD-ROM and DVD. Plus, many firms are turning to blended learning, combining classroom and online instruction. Online learning is booming, and will continue to grow, for everything from time management and leadership to technical skills and lead-generation training. Younger workers who've grown up in an online world increasingly will demand some type of e-learning because they're most comfortable with that form of content presentation.

It is unfortunate that many online business writing courses today are the one-size-fits-all variety. They don't always address the needs of all employees. Plus, the lack of real-time, personal interaction (and sometimes hand holding) may limit the effectiveness of online or other self-study courses.

If you've discovered that employees need only a refresher course on basic grammar and style, online training could work well. Many websites, including some affiliated with colleges, offer online classes covering these elementary skills, and they can be found through a simple Internet search. Fees usually are charged on a per-user basis.

Even for a basic grammar course, however, many employees prefer at least some classroom instruction where they can meet face-to-face with a trainer and ask specific questions. To determine the best learning method, weigh all the pertinent factors—locations where employees work, expertise of in-house instructors, budget available for outside instructors, average age of staff, and your own instincts about what would produce the best outcome.

Here are some specific learning methods that can be mixed and matched to suit the needs of your employees:

◆ classroom training
◆ e-learning or self-study programs
◆ one-on-one coaching
◆ continuing education classes at area schools.

During my workshops, usually with 15 to 20 people, about half frequently are raising their hands, pointing out corrections to the intentional mistakes on the screen, or sharing their versions of an exercise's rewritten paragraphs. Others, however, prefer not to share their writing out loud. These reluctant individuals feel more comfortable discussing their writing challenges in a one-on-one meeting or phone call with the trainer.

Even those willing to share their text in a group workshop reap huge benefits from individual meetings. These sessions enable every participant to address specific writing issues that trouble them: getting started, being wordy or stilted, gathering their thoughts into an organized whole, and much more. Many of my students have told me through evaluations or immediately after the sessions how much value they got from the personalized attention.

If you're holding half-day workshops, one-on-one sessions can be held on the same afternoon or about a week later. For full- or multiday programs, schedule the individual coaching one to two weeks later, either in person or over the phone.

If the instructor is incorporating one-on-one consultations, request sample documents from each participant two to three weeks before the group workshop. Documents can range from internal emails and meeting reports to performance reviews and new business proposals. Limit the number of pages to four or five so it's not too much work for the instructor. Someone in the company should ensure that these documents are delivered to the instructor by email or fax on a timely basis. At the outset, tell enrollees that emailing sample documents is *required* to complete the course, and remind them to delete any proprietary information that the trainer doesn't need to know to evaluate the writing.

Getting sample documents in advance gives the trainer time to review them and to discuss key areas of improvement with each employee. As part of the group workshop, the instructor might assign a document to be reviewed later during the one-on-one meetings.

Design a Writing Training Program

For classroom or blended learning, select one or more instructors, either from within the organization or from an outside training company. First consider the expertise already available to you in your learning or HR department, where staff members are somewhat familiar with employees' strengths and weaknesses. If one of the in-house trainers has some experience teaching writing, she or he could be an ideal choice. Another resource could be the corporate communications or public relations department, staffed by those whose job it is to write for the company. Some of these workers may be former journalists who know how to write the concise text that's needed in a business environment. When you approach these potential resources, keep in mind that being able to *do* and being able to *teach* are separate skills. Your ideal resource can do both. Also realize that you're asking people to take on an extra task in addition to their regular workload. Will they be willing to put time into designing training for employees who are not in their department? It may take a senior executive to make that happen.

The people you engage to train your employees should work with representatives from the learning/HR departments and with managers of those employees taking each of the planned courses to develop the instruction. If your trainers will be part of the communications/PR department staff, they also should consider developing a writing course specifically designed for those in their own department, focusing on documents such as press releases, newsletter articles, annual reports, and website communication.

If in-house trainers are not available or if the decision makers believe they don't have the expertise to teach business writing, then consider hiring an outside instructor. Find them the same way you find other trainers—through referrals, articles in the local business and trade press, and through the local chapter of ASTD.

Ask the instructor candidates to submit information about themselves along with references and links to their websites. Review their websites to see if they include a presentation video. Where possible, choose an instructor with experience in your industry or a related industry. Be sure the person is willing to tailor the course to the needs of the participants.

Be sure to speak to your candidates, either in person or over the phone, before signing a contract. Although email is a great tool for written information, it doesn't reveal a person's oral communication style. If you're hiring someone to teach your employees, you should listen to how he or she comes across and let your instincts tell you if the person is a good fit for your firm.

After you've hired an outside instructor, work closely with that person and with the participants' key supervisors to design training customized for the enrollees. Start by settling some of these issues:

- number of employees to be trained
- titles/job functions of those registered for the training (this will tell you how similar or different their needs are)
- documents that trainees frequently write
- patterns of particular writing problems (for example, vague language, wordiness, poor grammar) and how those problems hurt the firm
- extent and nature of writing instruction the trainees have had
- trainees' attitudes about their jobs and about learning (for example, do they see writing skill as material to their work or success; did they register willingly or were they told by a supervisor to do so?)
- corporate culture and how much writing is emphasized and valued.

You and the instructor(s) also should establish the following details:

- number of training hours (half day, full day, several days)
- size of each group (best to limit classes to 20 people)

- different types or levels of employees participating
- follow-up method
- availability of one-on-one consultations in addition to the group training.

Work with the instructor to develop a program ideally suited for those who are registered. Plan to sit in on the training to get a firsthand look at how employees are interacting and whether the instructor is connecting with them. Use your observations to make needed changes in the course work, the training methods used, and the instructor's approach.

Start promoting the writing program a few months in advance—perhaps while you're still selecting the instructor(s). Use vehicles such as internal printed and e-newsletters, blast emails, the company intranet, announcements at other courses, and payroll stuffers. And don't forget the all-important word-of-mouth advertising.

Follow Up to Maximize Training Results

A half-, full- or multiday workshop combined with one-on-one consultations can enhance employees' skills in several areas and give them more confidence as business writers. In an ideal world, these benefits will last indefinitely. But some employees may revert to poor writing habits a few weeks after the training. That's why follow-up is so valuable, either through additional training or consultations or via email.

You might instruct each participant to email the instructor another document (preferably one the employee actually is working on) about 30 days after the workshop. The instructor should review each document and email the employee a written critique that points out areas of improvement from earlier documents as well as problems that still need to be addressed. The "track changes" or "redlining" feature in most word-processing program should be used to reveal the edits made by the instructor. The employee should be able to call the instructor to discuss the critique because some issues are better addressed personally to avoid confusion.

In a perfect world, additional documents should be emailed at 30- or 60-day intervals throughout the year, but other priorities often make this impossible. You might arrange for the instructor to be available on an as-needed basis for employees to call or email.

Create a Corporate Culture That Values Good Writing

In addition to writing training conducted by one or more qualified instructor(s), your company needs to show employees that it stresses—and perhaps even rewards—good writing. Doing so starts with the owners and top executives using any means available to convey the importance of writing and to establish a noncompetitive atmosphere around writing. Plus, they should encourage employees to assist each other in reviewing and proofreading documents and to offer constructive criticism.

Expectations about writing should be published in the employee handbook, on the company intranet, and in other appropriate places. These notices should explain that, at a minimum, employees must write at a level of proficiency adequate for their job functions, based on clear standards the organization establishes for different types of documents. The notices also should explain that employees must be prepared for periodic evaluations of their writing by supervisors, including during performance reviews.

A section that should be in every organization's handbook is one that discusses business emails, stressing that they are to be treated like any other document—with logical organization and proper grammar, punctuation, and word usage.

Don't convey the company's emphasis on good writing as a threat because that would create even more angst for new employees and those not confident about their writing abilities. Instead, the company should reiterate regularly its commitment to excellence in communication—and point out that each employee is expected to own that commitment personally.

Link Good Writing with Leadership and Advancement

Many organizations invest heavily in training employees at various levels (from principals to first-line managers) to become better leaders. Presidents, chief executive officers, and other top executives need to articulate a clear vision for the company to as many as several thousand employees or more. They need to craft messages that help workers feel better about the firm and their jobs. In some cases, they need to explain why an unpopular change—such as the selling off of a division—is right for the company and ultimately will benefit most of the workforce (if that's the case). Much of this communication is through the written word—emails, internal newsletters, postings on the intranet, and other vehicles.

Mid-level and first-line managers are called on repeatedly to write and send to their subordinates emails and memos discussing new projects or procedures, work responsibilities, directives from upper management, goals, and other subjects. They also have the difficult task of writing documents that point out mistakes or recap for an employee a conversation about a disciplinary problem. The words and sentences they choose in all these types of documents will go a long way in determining how much respect and loyalty they engender among their subordinates. (See "Writing to Subordinates" in Step 7.)

Managers at various levels and would-be managers can ruin their opportunities for advancement if they continually write documents that are unclear, riddled with grammar mistakes, or offensive to their subordinates or—worse—clients. When a decision maker sees a pattern of poorly written or ineffective documents, he or she may decide that the writer isn't qualified to take the next career step.

By writing effectively, people at all levels of the firm can demonstrate that they

- clearly understand the problem or situation
- see how it affects the big picture of the organization
- can recommend logical, easy-to-follow next steps

- can explain who should do what going forward
- empathize with subordinates.

Those abilities are the hallmarks of successful leadership.

Poor writing also can short-circuit careers for candidates seeking managerial jobs who can't articulate on their résumés what they bring to the table. Too many job-seekers simply list previous employment and responsibilities without explaining their accomplishments (especially in a leadership role)—but that's exactly what most prospective employers want to know. And many job-hunters write dull cover letters, thus missing an opportunity to convey their most significant accomplishments as managers, their special leadership skills, their knowledge of the industry, and other qualities that employers look for.

Establish Companywide Writing Style Standards

One way to make employees immediately more comfortable about how they should write when speaking for or about the company is to create a style guide. This guide sets the rules for general grammar, punctuation, and word usage; it establishes official spelling, capitalization, and hyphenation rules to be followed in all documents produced by anyone in the company; and it describes the preferred design and organization for the documents most commonly produced. A style guide sets a corporate communications image that is easy to keep, and it takes much of the anxious uncertainty out of writing.

Here are some rules your corporate style guide could include:
- For numbers, spell out *zero* to *nine,* and use numerals for *10* and above.
- For numbers in the millions or higher, express in a decimal format ($7.5 million instead of $7,500,000). Naturally, financial reports with tables in which exact amounts are presented would be an exception to this rule.

- For names, use both the given name and the surname at the first reference; use the last name for all subsequent references. Avoid courtesy titles like *Mr., Miss, Ms.,* or *Mrs.*
- Write time in numeral format: 10 a.m., 7:30 p.m.
- Use two-letter standard postal abbreviations for states (NY, CA, OH, and so forth).
- To avoid reader confusion with acronyms, spell out the name or phrase the first time it is used and enclose the acronym in parentheses immediately following the spelled-out term. Here's an example: *We're committed to improving our return-on-investment (ROI).*
- Do not use all-caps type for the regular text portion of any document. Use all-caps type sparingly in headlines because it is more difficult to read.
- Use standard round bullets, indented five spaces from the left-hand margin.

That list is far from exhaustive. Draft a guide that answers the needs of your employees and is pertinent to your most frequently written documents. The guide shouldn't drive employees crazy with seemingly insignificant rules; instead, it should help workers stop wasting time trying to decide whether to capitalize the *D* in *Accounting Department.*

And remember that the style guide is a living document—it should be updated periodically as new questions arise or new documents become part of the corporate mix. One person or a team in the learning or HR department might be assigned the task of creating the new rules and continually updating the guide.

Also as part of the style guide, you may wish to add document templates and boilerplate language for standard documents. A template establishes the "look" of a document—the typefaces used for text and headlines, the margins, the layout for charts or tables, and so forth. Boilerplate language is standard wording that employees can pick up off the central server and update with data pertinent to the communication at hand. For example, an employee first would download the boilerplate language for a letter to a customer acknowledging receipt of a complaint. Then she or he would plug in the complaint details, the solution details, and other pertinent information before sending the letter.

Encourage Submissions to Company Publications

To further encourage your workers to hone their writing skills, invite employees at all levels to submit articles to the company's printed or emailed newsletter, the company intranet, or any other publications the firm produces. Consider offering incentives, such as gifts, additional vacation time, or cash for the best-written pieces. Ask for shorter rather than longer articles—these will help employees improve their editing skills and they're preferred by most readers in the impatient business world.

Stress Straightforward Language for ESL Employees

Many students who grew up speaking and writing a language other than English tell me about the difficulty inherent in learning English. They point to the many different words that mean about the same thing (such as *terrific, great, wonderful, excellent, marvelous, remarkable, super*), and the words that sound the same or are spelled almost the same but have completely different meanings or pronunciations (*here, hear; we, wee; bough, cough, dough, rough*). English as a second language (ESL) is no breeze.

For your ESL employees, building a strong and diverse vocabulary and understanding all the rules of the language may be an enormous challenge. One advantage that non-native speakers may have is in selecting simple words to convey their thoughts. Because they're not weighed down with a vast array of subtly different English words, they're more likely to keep their words simple and direct. That's the worthy goal for all business writers, no matter what language they communicate in: get readers to understand the message and take the desired action.

Despite the benefits of a less complicated vocabulary, it can be difficult for ESL employees to write effectively, especially in an environment where most of their co-workers have spoken and written English all their lives. Many non-native speakers overuse passive verb forms and arrange their words awkwardly in sentences that more closely resemble the sentence structure of their native language.

Writing training programs for these employees should focus on clarity with straightforward language and basic organizational skills.

Your Turn

Improving the writing quality across your company or organization requires a commitment of time and, if an outside instructor is retained, money. Before planning a writing training program, answer these questions to help determine your needs:

1. Are internal and external emails written with professionalism, clarity, and a tone appropriate for the readers?
2. Are all types of documents written with reasonably good grammar and a minimum of spelling mistakes and typos?
3. Are employees confused by the direction given in internal documents written by their managers and other co-workers?
4. Do writers get to the point quickly to engage the readers?
5. Are documents easy to read and well organized?

If you answered "no" to two or more of those questions, you should consider developing a writing training program.

RESOURCES

American Society for Training & Development. 2006. *Bridging the Skills Gap: How the Skills Shortage Threatens Growth and Competitiveness... and What to Do About It*. Alexandria, VA: ASTD Press.

Carter, Bonnie, and Craig States. 1996. *The Rinehart Handbook for Writers,* 4th edition. Orlando, FL: Holt, Rinehart and Winston.

The Forbes Book of Great Business Letters. 2001. New York: Black Dog & Leventhal.

Goldstein, Norm. 2004. *The Associated Press Stylebook*. New York: Basic Books.

Stovall, James Glen. 2006. *Writing for the Mass Media,* 6th edition. Boston: Pearson Education.

Strunk, William Jr., and E. B. White. 2000. *The Elements of Style,* 4th edition. Needham Heights, MA: Allyn & Bacon.

Zinsser, William. 2006. *On Writing Well,* 30th anniversary edition. New York: HarperCollins.

Helpful Websites

Resource: ACT: "WorkKeys Business Writing"
Description: Business writing tips, tests, and examples of common usage and grammar errors
Contact information: http://www.act.org/workkeys/assess/bus_writ/index.html

Resource: Capital Community College Foundation: "The Guide to Grammar and Writing"
Description: Explanations of grammar rules, indexed within categories
Contact information: http://grammar.ccc.commnet.edu/grammar/

Resource: Edufind: "Online English Grammar"
Description: Explanations of grammar rules, listed in alphabetical order
Contact information: http://www.edufind.com/english/grammar/toc.cfm

Resource: The Owl at Purdue: "Workplace Writers"
Description: Writing help and teaching resources, including tips for writing different types of documents
Contact information: http://owl.english.purdue.edu/owl/resource/681/01/

INDEX

Jack E. Appleman is an award-winning writer with more than 20 years' experience as a trainer, PR/communication professional, and professor. As president of SG Communications (http://www.sg writing.com), he conducts writing workshops that enable corporate employees at all levels to write more productively. Among the many articles Appleman has published was a column titled "Writing Instruction Helps PR Pros Break Through to the Media" (*PR Tactics and The Strategist Online*), which earned him a Business Marketing Association 2007 Impact Award. His other articles have addressed the importance of clear and concise writing. He also speaks frequently on writing and communication skills.

In his career, Appleman has written copy and supervised other writers creating press releases, technical articles, proposals, new business letters, and PowerPoint presentations. These efforts have helped many companies achieve their communication goals.

As a professor, Appleman teaches writing and communication courses at Fairleigh Dickinson University and William Paterson University, both in New Jersey. He also teaches continuing education-credit classes on business writing for insurance producers and offers one-on-one writing coaching.

He received his bachelor of arts in communication from Ohio State University, Columbus, and his master of science degree in journalism from Ohio University, Athens. Appleman earned the Certified Business Communicator (CBC) designation from the Business Marketing Association (BMA). He is a past president of BMA's New Jersey chapter and serves as vice president of marketing for the northern New Jersey chapter of the American Society for Training & Development.

Appleman lives with his wife Rosa and daughters Gail and Sarah in Monroe, New York, in the beautiful Hudson Valley region.